7 Steps to Success

Prem P. Bhalla

GOODWILL PUBLISHING HOUSE®
B-3 RATTAN JYOTI, 18 RAJENDRA PLACE
NEW DELHI-110008 (INDIA)

Published by
GOODWILL PUBLISHING HOUSE®
B-3 Rattan Jyoti, 18 Rajendra Place
New Delhi-110008 (INDIA)
Tel. : 25750801, 25820556
Fax : 91-11-25764396
E-mail : goodwillpub@vsnl.net
website : www.goodwillpublishinghouse.com

Printed at : Kumar Offset Printers, Delhi-92

Contents

Preface

God made everyone to succeed in life. Yet only one out of twenty people succeed. The others continue to live a life of mediocrity, blaming their own circumstances, the people around them and God for giving them a raw deal.

Success is a habit. All successful people understand and follow simple rules of living that contribute to their success. This small minority did not reach great heights because they were more fortunate than others. To wait for luck to smile upon them would have been like waiting for the impossible to happen. It would have been a needless waste of time and effort. They knew that it would be of no avail to close their eyes to reality. They had a life to live. They had to make the best of it.

Success begins in the mind as a thought. It may seem to be an insignificant idea. But ideas are like little newborn babies. At the time of birth, no one can tell how many of these little babies will attain eminence in their field of work and life. In the same way, when a thought is worthwhile, it soon becomes a dream. This dream, in turn, becomes the driving force to make a person act. Actions, when repeated, become habits, a way of life.

Positive actions help develop good habits, which are the foundation of success. This book, **Seven Steps to Success**, takes you step by step to the ultimate goal of making success your constant companion. Once you have learnt the art of success, you will wonder why people fail to succeed.

The wonderful world of success is open to everyone. It is for all those who are willing to make the effort to learn the easy rules that take one towards the goal. It is for all those who have faith in their abilities, and are willing to use them to make success a part of life.

— Prem P. Bhalla

What is Success?

What does success mean to you? Does it mean having lots of money? One's own luxurious home. A new car? Fame? A title? Many friends?

Success could mean one of these things. It could also mean something else, depending upon how one looks at it. There are many who have attained these, and a little more, and yet many people would not be willing to call them successful. There is certainly something more to it.

What then is success? The dictionary defines success as an achievement of an objective or a goal. Success can also mean attaining of a certain level of social status. Some define it simply as the opposite of failure. This would be a negative interpretation of success. Why compare it with failure when achieving success is our sole objective?

To a progressive person, success means the ability to realise oneself through one's everyday activities. To them, it is the ability to be able to live up to one's own expectations. There is an element of personal satisfaction in it. The success must be compatible with the true inner self. There must be balance in various spheres of life. Only when a person enjoys being alive, and likes the surroundings, can one be said to be truly successful.

SUCCESS AND HARD WORK

Success does not come only through hard work. There are people who have laboured all their lives, yet lived in poverty. Who could be more hardworking than a labourer who toils from morning till the evening only with brief interludes of rest? At the end of the day, he is handed over a small wage, barely enough to sustain himself and the family. That could not normally be labelled success.

Just because success cannot be achieved only through hard work, it does not mean that hard work is unnecessary or dispensable. There is no substitute for hard work. Success ultimately comes only through hard work. Only the hard work must be correctly directed. Besides, it must take into consideration various other elements that together lead to success.

SUCCESS AND MONEY

Success does not come from having lots of money either. Many people, who have inherited huge estates, or earned lots of money, complain that with all the wealth they still feel incomplete. It is true that to many people, money is a symbol of success. Yet, those who have it have never really found it wholly worthwhile. To them, money is a means to an end, but not an end in itself.

Those who accept money as a symbol of success, place it on a pedestal to be revered throughout their lives. Money is an obsession for them. They earn and hoard more money. A day arrives when they realise that their efforts were misguided. It is too late when they finally appreciate that *money is a good slave, but a poor master*.

SUCCESS AND POSSESSIONS

The basic purpose of earning money and accumulating it is to be able to buy comforts and possessions that are considered to be symbols of success.

On taking a close look at ourselves we begin to appreciate that we have very few real needs. We need simple food to survive. We can sleep only on one bed. We do not require a very big house either. We also realise that a small car can take us to our destination just as a big luxurious car can. We also appreciate that we do not require many of our possessions, purchased at the spur of a moment, more because of the thrill the experience provided rather than the need it fulfilled.

Yet human nature compels people to build and live in large homes, buy items of luxury, drive cars that are status symbols, and boast of their possessions to friends and others to seek recognition for having achieved "success". Many are impressed by the show of these possessions.

However, a time comes when one realises that the happiness these possessions give is momentary and short-lived. Possessions are undoubtedly symbols of success. Unfortunately, we give them undue importance and chase them without thought of personal need. This tilts the balance of life in one direction, creating confusion and disharmony.

Think it over...

"Too many people spend money they haven't earned, to buy things they don't want, to impress people they don't like."

— *Will Smith*

SUCCESS AND POSITION

Many people associate success with the attaining of certain positions at the workplace and in society. The higher a position one attains at work, the greater the prestige attached, and also the feeling of success. In the same way, people strive hard to attain positions in clubs, organisations and societies to gain recognition. Positions in politics are equally symbolic of success. People make great efforts to be elected as Municipal Councillors, and members of the legislative bodies at the state and national level. The race continues to seek appointments in special positions as committee chairpersons, ministers and may be the head of the state.

Titles too are symbols of success. In every field, titles are used not only to honour people, but also to motivate them to strive for higher positions and titles. The British used titles lavishly in the defence sector, in sports and public life. This was their way to keep people satisfied with their symbols of success.

This has continued even after India attained independence. Rather, the trend has only increased. The supervisor looks forward to be called an assistant manager, just as an assistant manager desires to be called a manager. The chain goes on with each person eyeing the next higher position. We see this in every field. In the armed forces, there are the lower ranks and the office cadres. The same is to be seen in the Police Services and the Administration Services. Even in the field of business and professions, we see titles as symbols of success. For instance, in the field of law, being called a 'Senior Advocate' is symbolic of a person having achieved success in that particular field.

Positions and titles are certainly symbolic of the level of success a person has achieved in a particular field. Like other forms of success, they are a source of joy and happiness. One enjoys great pleasure in them. But it is not long before one realises that this pleasure too is short-lived. What was success yesterday is not so today, because reaching the next higher position, or qualifying for the next higher title alone would now mean success to the individual. It continues to be a struggle to achieve further success. Besides, no position in life is permanent. One attains great heights only to step down some day.

Think it over...

Possessions, outward success, publicity, luxury — to me these have always been contemptible. I believe that a simple and unassuming manner of life is best for everyone, best both for the body and the mind.

— *Albert Einstein*

SUCCESS AND PEOPLE

Life is people. We deal with them every day everywhere — in our homes, at work and in the society. We are being observed all the time. The opinion people have of our abilities and activities influence our success. We are being tested all the time. It is the people who like to decide how successful we are in life.

There are two classes of people in this world. The first kind is the vast majority that lives by seeking each other's approval in every sphere of life. Each person tries to keep up with the other hoping that it will meet everyone's approval. To be surrounded by people who approve their activities means success to them. The second kind is a small minority who live by certain values and beliefs. Their conscience is their constant guide. Every time they are in doubt they look within for an answer. To them, success is being in harmony with their conscience.

WHAT IS SUCCESS?

We have just observed that hard work is necessary to succeed, but unless well directed, it may not lead one to success.

Money and material possessions are symbols of success, but may not necessarily have been acquired through honest, well-directed hard work. The joy and pleasure that one derives from these may not be lasting.

Positions and titles are definitely symbolic of success. Every individual seeks them. However, we have observed that one rises in life only to step down one day. It is the people in our life that make us aware of our success or failure. Therefore, it is natural for everyone to seek the approval of people that surround him or her at home, at work or in the society. However, not everyone may be well meaning. It is the individual's conscience that provides the ultimate answer.

In the ultimate analysis, since no two people are alike, how an individual perceives success may differ from one person to another. One perceives success when the achievements are in harmony with the personal desires. Since individual desires too will vary from one person to another, the people in our lives are bound to see and judge us from their point of view.

This makes it difficult for an individual to correctly appreciate the best form of success. The ideal form of success must fulfil the basic needs of an individual. It must promote self-esteem. Finally, it must touch all the fields of life — the home, the workplace and the society. One should not ignore personal needs either. The ideal form of success comes from living a balanced life.

OPPORTUNITIES FOR SUCCESS

Everyone is surrounded by opportunities, but only a few avail of them. Most people do not recognise opportunities. What exactly does one understand by the word “opportunity”? Is it a mysterious force that comes knocking at the doors of a blessed few? Is it the power to push and pull through life through recommendations of friends and relatives? Perhaps to some, it may mean a tailor-made job, or a flourishing business handed down from the family. To a few, it may mean the winning of the jackpot.

If an opportunity is one of these things to you, then, yes, opportunities are getting scarce. But that is not so.

Opportunities do not come knocking at our doors. They have to be created. An opportunity is no more then a fragment of a thought, which comes floating in the mind. We toy around with it. Through it we view a dream, shape it with our imagination and hard work, and gradually turn the dream into reality.

Contrary to popular belief, opportunities are not becoming scarce. They are constantly growing manifold. Each time a new discovery is made, or an invention perfected, it does not mean that yet another opportunity is closed. It means that many new opportunities are opening by way of jobs. Human beings have unlimited needs, and as long as there is a single human being on this earth, and he has needs to be fulfilled, there will be opportunities to fulfil them. Each opportunity beckons success.

WHAT LEADS TO SUCCESS?

Once several successful people were asked the simple question: What leads to success? Their answers can be simply summed up as under:

To succeed, one must:

1. Be willing to work hard.
2. Have great dreams.
3. Have skills, ability and talent.
4. Be honest and have integrity.
5. Be lucky.

These remarks are worthy of special notice:

"To be a really successful human being, you must have faith – in what you do and what you are." – *Clifford Grodd*

"To be successful, you have to be willing to make a commitment. – *Richard C. Auletta*

"I think success means being able to make other people's lives happier and easier, and I try for that. The key to life's success is balance…I think it is very important to work extremely hard." – *Frank Valenza*

"Success is more permanent when you achieve it without destroying your principles." – *Walter Cronkite*

In yet another survey, when people were asked what changes they desired in their lives, their answers revealed the following priorities:

1. Greater financial security.
2. Enjoy better health.
3. Achieve greater success.
4. Pleasant home life.
5. Attractive appearance.
6. Purposeful education.
7. Better family relationships.
8. Greater relaxation.
9. Better lifestyle.
10. Positive outlook on life.

Think it over...

Six essential qualities that are the key to success: sincerity, personal integrity, humility, courtesy, wisdom and charity.

— *William Meninger*

THE LAW OF SUCCESS

The desire to achieve can be traced back to the beginning of mankind. We have it on record what the saints and sages had to say about it more than 2500 years ago. The great philosophers and thinkers too have added valuable insights into the phenomenon of success. In the modern times, Napoleon Hill was one of leading thinkers to go deep into the issue. Over a period of over 20 years, he studied the lives of over 100 people, who were known for their outstanding success in different fields of life. Henry Ford, Thomas Edison, Dr. Alexander Graham Bell, Charles M. Schwab and John D. Rockefeller were few of the successful persons whose lives were studied in detail.

On the basis of this study, Napoleon Hill initially prepared a correspondence course that benefited thousands of eager young people. Later, it was put in the form of the popular book: The Law of Success, divided into 16 chapters, each covering one aspect of success.

Describing the elements of success, Napoleon Hill explained the importance of a pleasing personality, self-confidence, self-control, tolerance, a good imagination, and lots of enthusiasm. He emphasized that it was necessary to have a definite chief aim, which could be achieved through accurate thought, concentration and co-operation. The need to take initiative and develop leadership was important. He stressed upon the need for good teamwork that brings the benefits of the principle of the 'master mind' within the reach of an individual. He explained that successful people habitually delivered more than what they were paid for, and habitually made savings out of their earnings. Failure was as important part of life, as it was only a stepping-stone to success. Finally, he explained that we must treat others just as we would like to be treated by them.

SUCCESS AND HUMAN NEEDS

Human beings are driven by three distinct needs:

1. The need for self-preservation.
2. The need to carry on the human race.
3. The need for recognition, or power.

A need that is an offshoot of the third need is the need for money, which is symbolic of power.

Every individual desires success in fulfilling each of the above mentioned needs. Whereas the first need is symbolic of good health and a long life, the second need is symbolic of the need for a spouse, children and a home. Money is required to buy comforts for oneself and the family, and recognition is desired to promote self-respect and acceptance by the society.

The three human needs lead every individual to three distinct fields of activity in everyday life:

1. The family.
2. The workplace.
3. The society.

It is natural for every individual to desire success in each of these three fields of everyday activities. However, human nature is such that one tends to strive harder in one field at the cost of the other two, or may be strive in two fields at the cost of the third. Either way the balance between the three is lost. This way one fails to achieve the ideal success.

Maintaining a balance in different fields of everyday activities should be the prime concern of every person who desires to make success a constant companion.

SUCCESS AND THE FAMILY

Very few people realise that human needs cannot be fulfilled without a family. The institution of marriage and the family has withstood the test of time. The breakdown of the family has only given rise to newer problems.

With the growing economic freedom for women, many have challenged the need for marriage and the family. This has given rise to live-in relationships, single parents, adoptions and similar adjustments between men and women. Even within marriage, we witness promiscuity and extra-marital relationships, often leading to divorce and breakdown of a family. The affected men and women may justify such behaviour out of personal need, but ultimately, time catches on. Today there are more people than ever before who need psychiatric help because of marital and family problems.

Besides the adults involved in these fragile relationships, children have suffered enormously when they have not received the love and care that is the need of every child. From amongst the love-starved children, we see aggressive young people emerging, who are challenging the conduct of their parents. The broken families have given rise to great suffering and needless crime.

When a family works as a team, great things are achieved. A family begins with a young man and woman uniting in marriage to live a life together 'for better or for worse'. The secret of a happy marriage is commitment to the relationship. It aims at accepting the partner as an individual with personal hopes and aspirations. Both the partners fulfil definite responsibilities to create a team that achieves more than what the two individuals could attain separately.

When the children follow, it is important that both the parents must realise their responsibilities towards them. Many men feel that the mother needs to contribute more towards the upbringing of children, but experience has clearly shown that children coming from families where both parents contribute towards their upbringing are more balanced, and become responsible adults.

Money in the form of economic independence has emerged as the primary cause of marital conflicts and breakdown of the families. Many men and women are giving preference to earning more money rather than raise a happy, well-balanced family. These people fail to appreciate that just as money is a symbol of success, so is a happy family, a symbol of success. Money may contribute in adding to one's possessions, but it cannot buy either health or happiness. A happy family enjoys and provides both without cost.

> **Think it over...**
>
> Of course, there is no formula for success, except perhaps, an unconditional acceptance of life and what it brings.
>
> — *Arthur Rubinstein*

SUCCESS AT THE WORKPLACE

Irrespective whether one is in business or a profession, every individual spends almost one-third of the working adult life at the workplace. At the same time, it is at the workplace that one earns a livelihood. Money that one earns is a symbol of success. The position that one attains at work is also a symbol of success. This way success at the workplace is often gauged by one's position and the money earned. Both are motivating factors. One strives hard to attain both.

Success at the workplace begins with one's education. The better one is qualified, the higher the position one attains. Personal ability contributes significantly in qualifying for a better position and more money. While personal ability can be enhanced through knowledge and experience, an important aspect that contributes to one's success at the workplace is one's ability to handle human relationships.

At any workplace, there will be a variety of people – the seniors, colleagues and subordinates. At the same time, there will be customers and suppliers. Human beings have their own frailties, and success will depend upon how well one can understand and cope with these frailties in human relationships. The ultimate success will depend upon the image one creates upon the variety of people, both men and women one comes across at the workplace.

An individual's commitment at the workplace is yet another factor that will influence one's success there. Some people are so committed that they give their best to their vocation. They receive recognition for their efforts and even get more financial rewards, but if they cut on the time due to their family or the society, the balance begins to tilt in one direction. In the long run, this may not be appreciated. Whereas they may experience success at the workplace, they may be lacking in other fields.

Think it over...

Now in order that people may be happy in their work, these three things are needed: They must be fit for it; They must not do too much of it; And they must have a sense of success in it – not a doubtful sense, such as needs some testimony of other people for its confirmation, but a sure sense, or rather knowledge, that so much work has been done well, and fruitfully done, whatever the world may say or think about it.

— *John Ruskin*

SUCCESS AND THE SOCIETY

Besides the interaction with the family and at the workplace, no one can ignore the relationships that develop, as one becomes a part of the society or community. We build relationships with friends who stand by us, with the staff that looks after the building where we live, with teachers who teach our children, with salesmen who serve us at grocery and provision stores, and with a whole lot of other people who become a part of our lifestyle. Our relationships with these people influence the pattern of success we achieve.

People can make or mar your image. This explains how each individual is linked with the other. The larger the number of people who appreciate you in public, the greater your success in the society.

This motivates people to seek positions in public life. They strive to become office bearers in clubs and other organisations. They offer to look after the affairs of the building or the colony where they live. This makes them to seek to become Councillors in the Municipal Corporation, or become a member of the Vidhan Sabha or the Parliament. There are innumerable opportunities to become a part of the public life. Politics offers the greatest opportunity. People go all out putting in great effort and investing money to seek public approval to be elected to a position of respect and honour. This is symbolic of success. Attaining it fulfils a deep need within them.

Success in this field is addictive. Once a person enjoys it, there is need for more. It is an unending need. It is for this reason that people refuse to quit office. They want to hold on to the position for the great craving it satisfies within them. This craving is so great that once again individuals become so involved in it that they forget their responsibilities towards their families and even at the workplace. Their attention is focussed in one direction only. Whereas they may achieve success in this field, their success in the other two fields disturbs the overall balance of success in their lives.

YOUR QUESTIONS ANSWERED

CAN SUCCESS BE MEASURED?

Success must not be measured in terms of money, power, prestige, influence, education or standing in society. A man may have all of these and yet his life may be full of misery, unhappiness, moral corruption and ineffectiveness. Success must be measured by the yardstick of happiness, the ability to be happy and make others happy, the ability to be loved and to love, the ability to remain in peaceful harmony with those around you, with your own self and with God's cosmic laws.

— *Dada J.P. Vaswani*

BALANCED SUCCESS

An equitable success in the three major fields of activities in our lives is the best form of success an individual can enjoy. This makes it necessary that one must understand the responsibilities towards the family, at the workplace and in the society. One must fulfil these with love and care.

Many people feel that it is a tall order to fulfil. A person cannot possibly fulfil the many responsibilities involved. But successful people will tell you that you can achieve this, and yet more. You must rise above personal doubt.

Believe in your ability to achieve anything. God made everyone to succeed. If you are not prepared, now is the time to proceed to make success your constant companion.

Think it over...

Success is full of promises till men get it, and then it is as a last year's nest, from which the bird has flown.

— H.W. Beecher

POINTS TO PONDER

1. Hard work alone does not lead to success.
2. Money is a good slave, but a poor master.
3. The pleasure that possessions provide is short-lived.
4. One holds positions only to step down some day.
5. Success must be in harmony with one's conscience.
6. To be satisfying, success must touch all aspects of life.
7. One cannot wait for opportunities for success. They must be created.
8. Success comes from satisfying the basic human needs.
9. One must aim to attain balanced success.

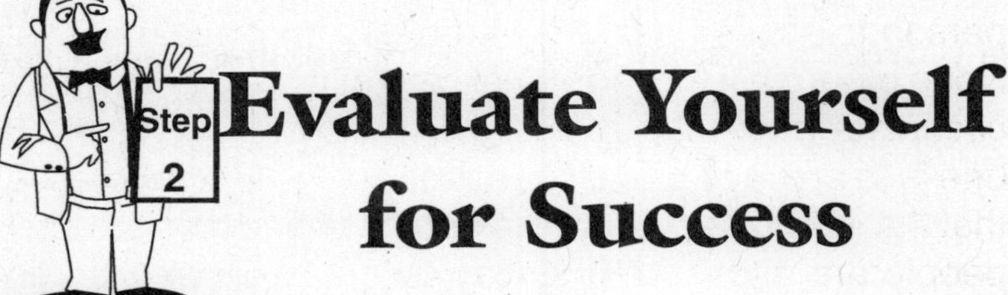

Evaluate Yourself for Success

Who knows you best? Your family? Your teachers? Your friends and colleagues? Or someone else?

Your teachers may have influenced the way you think. Your parents may have contributed to the value system you have adopted in life. Your friends and colleagues may have a certain amount of influence upon you. The truth is that no one knows you better than you. That makes you the best person to evaluate yourself, as you begin your journey to learn how to make success your constant companion.

A journey of a thousand miles begins with a single step. You begin from wherever you are today. You must know how well you are equipped. You must know what are your strengths. You also need to know what weaknesses need to be overcome, or what hurdles need to be crossed.

You will appreciate that every individual is born unique. For this reason, every individual responds differently to the circumstances. Even children born of the same parents, brought up under similar circumstances in the same home, and educated in the same school and college grow up to become very different kind of individuals. Few would accept this fact easily. Yet there are no two thoughts about it. People grow up to look at life and success differently.

Every individual, in his or her own right, is the best person to assess personal strengths and weaknesses. None other than the individual can truly gauge individual circumstances in the same light as one can personally. If one is to arrive at a realistic assessment, it is imperative that the individual must do an honest self-analysis. Many people are often carried away by others' opinions and wishful thoughts, rather than by facts.

YOUR IMAGE

What do people think of you? Different people may have varied opinions about you. Your wife and the family who know you intimately may have one impression about you, and the friends quite another. It is possible that people in general may have yet another opinion about you. What may appear stranger is that you may think very differently about yourself. This way it is obvious that you may be projecting many separate images of yourself.

The truth is that every individual is multifaceted, and seen as many persons put together. Most people are content as they are. However, a person who sees a purpose in life and desires to make success a constant companion cannot accept this. A conscientious, honest and straightforward person always endeavours to remove the parallax between the several images that may be projected inadvertently.

Different people may interpret the words and deeds of others to suit their personal convenience. However, many times the erratic actions of a person may project a variety of images. To ensure that it is not so, a person must review and amend actions to project a fair image. It is not enough to harmonize the actions with the image one wants to project. It is equally important to understand the many factors that affect the image quality. Also, how one can exercise the maximum control over them to gain personal advantage.

A good public image is not made up of a single act of great merit. Nor does it consist in possessing more material benefits than others possess. It is the sum of total effect created by the individual's thoughts, actions, habits, attitudes and personal philosophies. One's education, competence in business or profession, a pleasant home life, efficiency in meeting the challenges of the day, and many other factors affect the personal image. Few people are able to create a fair balance between these factors, but the sum total effect can be quite interesting.

Think it over...

Where do you want to go in life? How do you want to get there? Do the roles you fill contribute to your goal? What is really important that you do? What merely fills up time? In determining your best roles, keep those that advance you towards your goal and eliminate those that are useless and a drag. Your trouble may be too many roles. You cannot afford to take on more than you can handle well.

— *Henry R. Brandt*

INDIVIDUAL BEHAVIOUR

Why does an individual behave in a particular manner? This is because the basic characteristics, as inherited from the parents, react with the environment to shape the individuals. Living is a continuous process. Change is an integral part of it. Each day, every hour and minute of it, life is undergoing a change. Whether it is for the better or for worse depends upon how one reacts to the environment. Since no two persons have the same inherited characteristics, each one reacts differently to similar environments, and grows up to be an individual personality, unique in every way.

Life is a continuous struggle for existence. Only the fittest can make a mark in life. A baby may appear frail but he also learns to cope with the environments, which surround him. He has his own methods to draw attention and fulfil his needs. It is not possible to have all of one's desires fulfilled the way one may want. It becomes necessary to compromise with certain aspects of life. This becomes the cause of some anxiety and tension. How one copes with this anxiety and tension influences one's habits and attitudes, which eventually become a part of the individual.

Individuals are being constantly shaped. To cope with the circumstances and the anxieties and tensions, some react to become doers rather than thinkers. Many find peace in being alone, in being planners rather than executors. Others avoid tension by seeking perfection in everything. Some may prefer to be emotional or dramatic. We cannot ignore the weaker ones who may become suspicious, or those who may lean upon imaginary ailments to cope with the anxieties of living.

Some of these ways of living appear attractive, and others unpleasant. None of these is lastingly impressive, or useful, if adopted in the extreme form. Fortunately, most people are a mixture of different types, with one type predominating. This necessitates a thorough self-analysis. This can lead to adopting those habits and attitudes, which are useful in the given circumstances. To begin with this may seem difficult, but it becomes easy through learning and deliberate effort in the right direction.

SELF-ANALYSIS

A simple method to know where one stands today is to analyse one's strengths and weaknesses. This way one would know what strengths must be further developed, and also what weaknesses need to be overcome. This gives one an overall picture of one's personality.

However, most people are unable to analyse their feelings and attitudes immediately. They may know how they feel, but may not be able to express themselves in words, or on paper. They may fail to understand or describe the image they project. Qualified psychologists can make this work easier, but their services are not always available. To make it easier, a simpler approach would be to follow some of the methods described below.

Think it over...

To become an able and successful man in any profession, three things are necessary – nature, study and practice.

— *H. W. Beecher*

PERSONALITY TRAITS

Given below is an elaborate list of words that describe common personality traits and feelings found in people. The list is fairly exhaustive. Some more traits could be added, but the common ones are there. English has a large vocabulary. You will come across several words that seem to have similar meaning. However, each word has finer meanings. Select ones that describe you best. Ignore those that do not relate to you. If you are not sure of the meaning of a word, consult a dictionary. The words are in alphabetic order. They describe both the strengths and weaknesses in peoplé. Tick those that you feel describe you best.

Absent-minded
Adaptable
Aesthetic
Affectionate
Aggressive
Alert
Ambitious
Amiable
Anxious
Apprehensive
Arrogant
Artistic
Assertive
Attractive
Authoritarian
Autocratic
Beautiful
Boastful
Boisterous
Bold
Brave
Broadminded

Calm
Candid
Capable
Careless
Cautious
Charitable
Charming
Cheerful
Childish
Clumsy
Committed
Companionable
Compassionate
Competent
Complaining
Composed
Compulsive
Conceited
Confident
Conformist
Confused
Conscientious

Considerate
Contented
Convincing
Coolheaded
Co-operative
Cordial
Courageous
Courteous
Crazy
Creative
Critical
Crude
Cruel
Curt
Daring
Decisive
Dependable
Depressed
Detached
Devoted
Dictatorial
Diligent

Diplomatic
Disciplined
Discouraged
Discreet
Dishonest
Disillusioned
Disinterested
Docile
Dominant
Dramatic
Dreamy
Dull
Dutiful
Eager
Easily-hurt
Easy-going
Egoistic
Emotional
Encouraging
Enthusiastic
Erratic
Ethical
Evasive
Excitable
Failure
Faint-hearted
Fair
Faithful
Far-sighted
Fashionable
Fearful
Feeble
Fickle

Firm
Flamboyant
Flexible
Flimsy
Foolish
Forgiving
Formal
Frail
Friendly
Gaudy
Generous
Gentle
Genuine
Good-looking
Gorgeous
Graceful
Greedy
Gullible
Half-hearted
Handicapped
Handsome
Hardboiled
Hard-headed
Hardy
Haughty
Headstrong
Healthy
Helpful
Hesitant
Honest
Humane
Humble
Humorous

Hypocritical
Idealistic
Ignorant
Imaginative
Immature
Impartial
Impulsive
Inattentive
Incompetent
Indifferent
Indulgent
Industrious
Inefficient
Ingenious
Insensitive
insincere
Intellectual
Interfering
Inventive
Jittery
Just
Knowledgeable
Lavish
Lazy
Lenient
Liberal
Lively
Lonely
Loving
Magnanimous
Mature
Maudlin
Mean

Meek
Mellow
Merciful
Methodical
Meticulous
Mischievous
Moody
Motivated
Negative
Negligent
Nervous
Novel
Objective
Observant
Obstinate
Offensive
Officious
Orderly
Original
Ostentatious
Outspoken
Partisan
Patient
Pedantic
Performer
Persevering
Persistent
Persuasive
Pious
Placid
Plain
Pleasant
Polite

Positive
Precise
Pretty
Procrastinating
Proud
Prudent
Puerile
Pushing
Rash
Rational
Reasonable
Refined
Religious
Reluctant
Reserved
Resourceful
Responsible
Rigid
Romantic
Rude
Sacrificing
Saucy
Scrupulous
Secure
Self-confident
Self-conscious
Selfish
Sensible
Sensitive
Sentimental
Serene
Sharp
Shrewd

Shy
Simpleton
Sincere
Slavish
Sloppy
Slow
Smart
Smug
Sober
Sociable
Sophisticated
Spirited
Spiteful
Spontaneous
Sporting
Steady
Stern
Straightforward
Strict
Strong-willed
Stupid
Suave
Subjective
Submissive
Subservient
Successful
Superficial
Supportive
Suspicious
Sympathetic
Tactful
Talkative
Tame

Theatrical
Thoughtful
Thoughtless
Timid
Tolerant
Tough
Tranquil
Trendy
Trusting
Truthful
Unassuming
Unbiased
Uncertain
Unconcerned
Undisciplined
Undisturbed
Unethical
Unruffled
Upright
Vain
Versatile
Vindictive
Virtuous
Vivacious
Volatile
Vulgar
Wasteful
Weak-willed
Well-behaved
Wile
Winning
Witty
Worldly
Worrier
Zealous

This analysis is for your personal use. Once you have gone through the list, note down the words you have ticked in the list. Do it honestly in privacy. There will be several words that describe you and your feelings. Sort them in two groups. The first one should include words that describe your strengths. The second group should include words that describe your weaknesses. How does one differentiate between the two groups? You can do so by asking yourself what is the effect of the particular trait. If it contributes to your confidence, it is a positive trait. It adds to your strength. If it robs you of your confidence, it is a weakness. Together the two lists will help you understand yourself better.

Using the words in the two groups, write paragraphs to describe your strengths and weaknesses. You need to identify your strengths so that you could use them to make success your constant companion. The weaknesses would guide you about what you need to correct in your everyday life. It is not difficult for determined people to overcome their weaknesses.

> **Think it over...**
>
> Seek the counsel of men who will tell you the truth about yourself, even if it hurts you to hear it.

PERSONAL APTITUDES

Aptitude is a natural ability or tendency in an individual. Psychologists have been able to identify several aptitudes or abilities. With the help of specially devised tests, these can be measured in individuals. Based on these findings, positive suggestions can be made as to what a person needs to do to attain success in life.

Several interests and aptitudes have been found to predominate in individuals. It is not possible to analyse an individual without specific tests by a qualified psychologist. The only alternative is to go through the list of the common interests and abilities listed below. Underline those that you feel are applicable to you.

It is not necessary that one may excel in only one, two, or three aptitudes or abilities. One may be above average in a few, but may really be capable in as many as eight or nine of them. Underline or tick all those you can identify in yourself. List them on a piece of paper, in the order of importance to you. The first two or three should be taken to be your special strengths. The others would be of useful to develop hobbies and additional interests.

Ability for pitch discrimination	Ability to think in three dimensions
Ability to learn new words	Ability to use small tools

Aesthetic appreciation
Accounting ability
Artistic ability
Business interest
Clerical interest
Cultural conformity
Desire for attention
Desire for diversion
Interest in outdoor work
Interest in self-reliance
Love of adventure
Love of fantasy
Mechanical ability
Resistance to restriction
Scientific interest
Social ability
Social welfare interest

ABILITIES NECESSARY FOR SUCCESS

An individual's successes are always related to the abilities and skills one possesses. Those who are able and skilful always enjoy whatever they are doing. Those without ability drag their way through work. Since every individual is unique, the abilities and skills too vary from one person to another. Some abilities and skills come naturally. Others need to be learnt.

Listed below are abilities and skills that promote success in a variety of fields of life. Tick ones that you possess. Try to evaluate how you can use these skills to achieve greater success in life. If you are lacking in a particular field, you can take appropriate training and prepare yourself for complete success.

Ability to comfort people
Ability to handle crises
Ability to see in graphic form
Ability to take decisions
Above average creativity
Adaptable to changing circumstances
All-round knowledge
Analytical outlook
Appreciate composition and colour

Appreciate discipline in life
Appreciate need for secrecy
Can face stress and tension
Communication skills
Computer literacy
Enjoy self-confidence
Enjoy working with machines
Enjoy working with numbers
Fond of reading
Fond of upgrading skills
Get along well with people
Good etiquette and manners
Good health and physique
Good imagination
Good knowledge of one's field
Good language skills
Good leadership qualities
Good listening skills
Good memory for names and faces
Good observation
Good speaking skills
Good team member
Good writing skills
Have an eye for unscrupulous people
High intellectual ability
Highly quality conscious
Highly self-motivated
Integrity and honour
Love for adventure and fun
Love for animals
Love for nature and outdoors
Not easily discouraged
Pleasing personality
Possess an aesthetic sense
Possess special artistic skills
Ready to work with own hands
Respect for time
Sense of showmanship
Sensitive to others' problems
Sincere and service-minded
Thorough and methodical
Understands shapes and figures
Vision to see ahead
Willing to take responsibility
Willing to try new ideas
Willing to work in different locations
Willing to work late at odd hours

> **Think it over...**
>
> Be studious in your profession, and you will be learned. Be industrious and frugal, and you will be rich. Be sober and temperate, and you will be healthy. Be in general virtuous, and you will be happy. At least, you will, by such conduct, stand the best chance for such consequences.
>
> — *Benjamin Franklin*

PERSONAL FEELINGS

No person who ignores personal feelings can achieve success. It is therefore necessary that one must analyse personal preferences, aptitudes and attitudes. The strengths and weaknesses must be duly considered. This can best be done only by the individual, who is aware of both the deep-rooted hopes and aspirations one may cherish, and also the limitations that hold one back.

The process of self-analysis must be ruthlessly realistic. One can be dishonest with somebody else and get away with it. When one's future is involved, one personally suffers for it. Therefore, one must always analyse personal feelings in strict honesty.

Simply thinking of your feelings and attitudes is not sufficient for self-analysis. You need to note down your reactions. Here are a few questions. As you answer them, there is much that you will learn about yourself.

THE FAMILY BACKGROUND

Take a look at your family background. Then answer these questions honestly:

- Would you call your childhood a happy period of your life?
- Are you carrying any childhood memories that still hurt or haunt you?
- Does an atmosphere of general welfare and success exist within the family?

YOUR CAPABILITIES

- How do you rate your personal capabilities? How do you rate yourself?
- What do you think about your education?
- Are you working to acquire the knowledge that would help you gain success in the fields of your choice?
- How do you rate your learning habits?
- What kind of newspapers and magazines do you read?
- How many and what kind of books do you read each year?

YOUR PHYSICAL AND EMOTIONAL SELF

- How is your health? Is it good, or are you prone to ailments like coughs and cold?
- Is any aspect of your health of special concern to you?
- Are there any areas of emotional conflict in your life?
- Are you in full control of yourself?

- Do you have any hobbies?
- Are they useful to you?

PERSONAL RELATIONSHIPS

Your relationships with people can be an important guide in assessing how well you can get along with others.

- Do you make friends quickly, or do you have more acquaintances than friends?
- Are you outgoing, or do you prefer relationships with a few, reliable friends?
- Does interaction with people bring you happiness, or stress?

YOUR CAREER

- Are you involved in a worthwhile career?
- Are your personal attitudes in harmony with those required by the career you have selected?
- Are you mentally capable and prepared to meet the challenges that your career will offer you?

YOUR STRENGTHS

- What are the areas of your personal strength?
- How can you develop your strengths further?
- Do you know how to use them to attain success?

YOUR LIMITATIONS

- Have you any personal limitations?
- Can you overcome these limitations?
- How, and by when?

YOUR FIELD OF CHOICE

In which field of activity are you most comfortable?

- The home and family?
- The workplace?
- The society?

Do not answer these questions in a hurry. Take your time over them. Think about them. Give due thought to every aspect of your personality. Note down the answers in a notebook. Does the picture that emerges from the answers match with the picture you have of yourself?

YOUR SUCCESSES AND FAILURES

There is yet another method of self-analysis. On a sheet of paper, write down what you consider to be your achievements in the past. What personal abilities and skills contributed towards each success?

In the same way, make another list in which you can note down occasions when you failed to achieve what you had set out to do. Against each, note down which of your bad qualities betrayed you.

You would now have a list of both your abilities and skills that helped you succeed, and also those that let you down. Once you reach this stage, it is only a matter of further developing your strengths, and gradually getting over your weaknesses.

When you have assessed your past successes and failures, you will begin to appreciate why it is necessary to cultivate habits like good self-control, use of tact and understanding in personal relationships, following the middle path, positive thinking, being soft-spoken, and being thoughtful about others. These virtues contribute to developing self-confidence and building a good character. With bad habits like negligence, procrastination, indifference towards others, and irresponsible speaking, which lead to failure, gradually eliminated from everyday life, one is able to strive towards more successful living.

The shortest route to success is to develop those abilities and skills that have contributed to your past achievements. At the same time, get over those negative habits that have let you down.

Think it over...

The greatest results in life are usually attained by simple means and the exercise of ordinary qualities. These may for the most part be summed in these two — commonsense and perseverance.

— *Feltham*

LOOKING BACK

It is a blessing to have a happy childhood and adolescence. They are the best stepping-stones to success. Happy memories promote self-confidence and faith in the institution of the home and family. Unfortunately, only a few claim to be so blessed. The majority only looks back at the desires that could not be fulfilled. They grumble and complain about their circumstances.

We cannot choose our parents. It is also not possible to control the environment in childhood. Besides, nothing can be done about the time that has gone by. There is no point in crying over it. Just think about it.

If you are of the opinion that the past has been unkind to you, think about it again. It has been unkind because you *think* that it has been unkind. There are many like you. With so many affected, don't you think that it could be a normal thing in everyone's life? Why not accept it as normal, and use it as a stepping-stone to success in the future? When you allow the unhappy thoughts of the past to linger in your mind, you are unnecessarily robbing yourself of the vital strength that could be used to take you ahead. Bury your past grievances and move ahead. There is a better world waiting for you.

UNDERSTANDING YOURSELF

The purpose of self-analysis is to identify one's strengths and also to consider personal sensitivities and shortcomings. If you have been able to answer the questions about your own feelings and personality traits, interests and abilities, you are definitely in a better position to understand yourself better.

Just as an accountant draws a balance sheet to show the assets and liabilities of a business firm, you need to draw a personal balance sheet of your personal assets and liabilities as represented by your strengths and weaknesses. The more honest you are with your assessment, the more accurate your picture will be. You will do well to include in your assets, your family status and reputation, your personal appearance and physique, or other similar considerations. On the liability side, you will need to include personal sensitivities like lack of confidence, religious restrictions, secret fears, and other similar shortcomings.

Use the picture that emerges out of this exercise as a stepping-stone to greater success in life. Do not be discouraged by your shortcomings or weaknesses. The very fact that you have been able to identify them means that you are aware of them. You can make an effort to get over them. With an honest self-evaluation, you are ready to proceed to attain greater success in the fields of your choice.

Think it over...

It is not so much being free from faults and imperfections as overcoming them that is an advantage to us; it being with follies and weaknesses and errors, as with the weeds of a field, which, if destroyed on the soil where they grow, enrich and improve it, more than if they had never sprung up there.

— *Anon*

POINTS TO PONDER

1. Personal evaluation prepares a person to move ahead in life.
2. People may perceive you to be very different from what you may be.
3. The inherited characteristics and the environment exert an influence to shape individuals.
4. Self-analysis is not easy because of one's personal thoughts and feelings.
5. Getting to know one's personal traits helps one to self-analyse.

6. A variety of aptitudes and interests make every individual different.
7. The greater the number of personal abilities, the better the chances of success.
8. Individuals should not ignore their personal feelings.
9. One can learn a lot about oneself by answering simple questions about the family, capabilities, health, career, relationships and similar things.
10. Past successes and failures can provide important guidelines for the future.
11. Understand yourself better by reviewing your past.

Prepare Yourself for Success

After you have completed the self-analysis in more than one ways to gauge and understand your own abilities, aptitudes and feelings, you know where you stand today. You know what others think of you, and how you would like to be accepted. At this point, you are also aware of your strengths and limitations. It does not matter whether the analysis indicates that you are as good as you thought you were, or may be you have to strive harder to come up to your own expectations.

Do not compare yourself with others. We discussed earlier that each individual is unique. There never was one like you before, nor is there one like you today. Even in future, there will be none who will be exactly like you. Each one is at a different level of development. What you are today is how you reacted to the environments you were exposed to. The important thing is not what you are today, but what you want to be tomorrow. Life is dynamic. It is forever offering new challenges. Either you grow, or you decay. The choice is yours.

When you set out on your journey to prepare yourself for success, if you do not compare or compete with others, whom do you compare yourself with? How do you measure your own progress? You are your own “yardstick”. You measure your progress with what you are today. All that is expected of you is to improve upon yourself each day.

You may add on to your abilities or skills in whatever way you find it necessary. That is, you may add on to your strengths. In the alternative, you could also get over some of your own weaknesses or personal limitations. Either way, you prepare yourself for success.

Think it over...

The ability to accept responsibility is the measure of the man.

— *Roy L. Smith*

TAKE RESPONSIBILITY

Where do you begin to prepare yourself for success? You begin from wherever you are today. Your first step should be to take responsibility for what you are. It is common to hear complaints about why a person is not what he or she wanted to be. Some complain against the parents, the teachers, and the relatives, and others blame the circumstances, and of course, that "luck" never favoured them. They will blame everyone and everything, but not themselves.

Is that the correct way of looking at it? Could you not have changed the direction of your life by taking charge over it? When you do not take charge it is like setting out on sea without a rudder on your boat. Under such circumstances can you expect the boat to reach its destination? It will only go wherever the waves and the wind carry it.

You must immediately stop blaming the people and the circumstances in your life. When you blame others, you are shifting responsibility for your life on others. You are needlessly pointing an accusing finger. Why don't you appreciate that you came alone to this world? You will also be alone when you leave it. The people and circumstances came your way just as they do in everyone's life. It is time that you take responsibility for what you are today. When you take responsibility, it means that you are in control over yourself.

What does taking responsibility mean? In simple words, it means that henceforth, you will be responsible for both your successes, and also the failures. This is the only fair way of getting ahead. When you succeed, you will be benefited by it. In the same way, when you fail, you will suffer for it. Where do others come into the picture? This way, you will think before you act. You will want to be successful. You will also want to avoid failure.

Think it over...

If our purpose is honest, and our efforts are sincere, we cannot fail. Success is never handed out to anyone; it has to be earned by perseverance, hard work, energy, patience and singleness of purpose.

— Anon

SUCCESS CONSCIOUSNESS

To succeed in everyday life, one must develop success consciousness. You may be building a home, starting a business venture, standing for the general elections, or just planning a meeting of a group of friends to discuss an important issue. Before success can come your way, it must become a reality in your mind. A thought is a powerful force, and if one must make success a constant companion, every force must be put into action.

To achieve success, you must be consciously aware that you are capable of it not once, but every time. This self-confidence keeps generating a powerful force within a person. With success achieved mentally, each time when one gets into action, there is not only an advantage over others, but success comes almost automatically. On the contrary, if you only wish for success, you are unconsciously admitting that you are not capable of it. You can then get it only as a gift from God.

How does one develop success consciousness? There is only one way to achieve this. Your mind must desire for success all the time. When you desire it, you will get it. You must feed your mind with thoughts of success all the time. It may be difficult initially, but soon, success consciousness becomes a part of an individual, and then it happens almost without any effort.

Take a positive step towards developing success consciousness by adopting this resolution:

Resolution

I, ...

do hereby resolve to develop my abilities and skills everyday to make success my constant companion.

Display this resolution on your working desk where you can see it everyday. Or paste it on the mirror of your dressing table. Let your family members, relatives and friends know about your resolution. This way they will keep reminding you about what you have set out to do. Each reminder will only help your resolution to go deeper into your subconscious to make success consciousness a part of you.

YOUR HABITS

You are what your habits make you. It is through habits that one projects an image to the people. Habits can be both, good and bad. When good habits predominate, one is called good. On the other hand, people with bad habits are always avoided. Good habits are important to a person who wants to make success a constant companion.

Habits are not formed overnight. They are the result of repeated actions. With each repetition, the action gets ingrained deeper into the subconscious until it becomes a habit.

In childhood, one wonders how a bicycle can balance on two wheels. When one learns to ride it, it is not without making many mistakes, loss of balance, lack of coordination and similar faults. Initially, when towards balancing the bicycle, one fails to control the handle bar. If one concentrates on the handle bar, one may lose hold of the pedals and the bicycle may come to a halt. The actions are gradually ingrained into the subconscious so that one balances the bicycle, controls the handle bar and also constantly moves the pedals to keep the bicycle moving. Later, one develops enough control to carry passengers on the pillion, and drive through narrow lanes in tight traffic. Once a person learns how to ride a bicycle, even after a gap of several years, one can still ride a bicycle. The ability and technique lie deep within the subconscious.

Learning to drive a scooter or a motorcycle is similar to learning how to ride a bicycle, but involves additional skills of controlling the speed on a road that may offer greater challenges. Driving a car offers other kinds of challenges like controlling the clutch with one foot, and the brake and accelerator with the other. At the same time, while one handles the gear-stick with the left hand, one controls the steering wheel with the right hand. The eyes have necessarily to be on the road. With some practice, one is not only able to do all this, but one also talks and looks around while moving at a fairly high speed.

Just as one learns to drive almost effortlessly through repetition and practice, one can develop habits that promote efficiency and goodwill and help attain success.

A habit is formed when an action is repeated day after day. Every action is the result of a thought. It is the thoughts that control the actions. Positive thoughts lead to positive actions. Similarly, negative thoughts lead to negative actions. Every individual desires that there should only be positive thoughts, but this is not possible. The quality of thoughts is dependent upon one's parents, the upbringing, teachers and education, friends and other influences. This does not mean that a person does not have control over the thoughts. The reality is that most people are so conditioned by the past experiences and the surroundings that they fail to exercise their own control over the thoughts. It is also true that most people do not know or understand the truth about how people think. They fail to realise that thoughts are the foundation of habits, and of success that one desires in life.

YOUR THOUGHTS

Thoughts are the foundation of all habits, and also of change. You will do well to understand how they influence everyday life and success.

Most of us ignore our thoughts, taking them to be something that comes fleeting through the mind only to please or displease us momentarily. All thoughts are important. They must not be ignored or overlooked. They are catalysts of change, either for good or bad. They are like seeds. From these seeds, plants grow in the form of words. These plants bear fruits in the shape of actions. We have already seen how repeated actions become habits.

We could also compare thoughts with drops of water. Every little drop accumulates till the utensil fills up. Once full, it spills over. In the same way, thoughts accumulate in the mind. They overflow as words. These words lead to actions, and actions become habits.

It is interesting to note that good thoughts are accepted hesitatingly. For this reason, they spread very slowly. On the other hand, bad thoughts are easily available and also easily acceptable. Many willing people are available to propagate them.

Thoughts can be either positive or negative. Positive vibrations emerge from positive thoughts, and negative vibrations come from negative thoughts. Depending upon the kind of thoughts one nurtures in the mind, the quality of life is influenced accordingly. It takes an equal amount of effort to think positive or negative.

Friends and people have a profound influence over one's thoughts. Good thoughts emerge in the company of good people. Good thoughts are always deep-rooted and are backed by determination. They are not easily destroyed by the conflicts of everyday life. Everyone must sow the seeds of good thoughts. When the bad thoughts are eliminated, the evil and sin reduce proportionately.

We must appreciate how thoughts influence change. The change in thinking changes our beliefs. When we change beliefs, our expectations are changed. This, in turn, changes our attitudes. The change in attitude influences one's behaviour. This finally influences the actions, habits and life.

Think it over...

The happiness of your life depends upon the quality of your thoughts, therefore guard accordingly; and take care that you entertain no notions unsuitable to virtue and reasonable nature.

— *Marcus Antoninus*

CONTROLLING THOUGHTS

You are what your thoughts have made you. You may not have attained the success you may have desired because you may have only wished for it. If you truly want to succeed, believe in your ability. You will reach the height you believe you are worthy of attaining.

There is magic in believing. Whatever you believe, your mind conveys it to every part of the body. Thoughts of good health, success and happiness benefit every bit of you, and those with whom you come in contact. In the same way, negative thoughts of sickness, failure, hatred, greed and revenge also affect your life, though adversely.

If you have not been aware of the magic of belief in the past, you can make amends now. Make the effort to transform yourself. Visualize yourself as what you want to be. Believe in your ability to change. Do not wish for it. When you wish for success, you believe that you are inferior. It will not bring about good results.

Feeding the mind with positive and constructive thoughts helps develop personal power. When negative thoughts are entertained, there is a corresponding loss of power. The balance between the two decides what power one is capable of exerting. This makes the need for positive thinking obvious. Unfortunately, nineteen out of every twenty people lean towards the negative side of life. From this, it may appear that positive thinking is difficult to practice. This is not so. The truth is that it is as easy to think positively as it is to think negative. Only the people fail to understand this.

The difference lies in the individual attitude. Thoughts become actions, and actions when repeated turn into habits. These, in turn, influence our attitudes and the environment, which conditions our minds. With an overwhelming majority already in the grip of negative thoughts, habits, and attitudes, the environment too gets charged with a high dose of negativity. This vicious circle goes on.

Every individual is constantly receiving suggestions, of both a negative and a positive nature from the environment. With a higher incidence of negativism, the suggestions are more negative than positive, and so is our receptivity.

Try an experiment to study the influence of suggestions on a person. Plan it so that four or five persons meet him at intervals, at different times of the day, and each time let the person point out that he is looking run-down, and perhaps needs to consult a doctor. By evening, he will really want to go to the doctor.

The reverse is also true. A student takes greater interest and scores well in a subject when a teacher repeatedly suggests that he has a natural aptitude for the subject. In the same way, actors put in greater effort when they are told that their acting is true to life. In a similar way, a soldier fights unmindful of the risk to his life because he believes that he is the fittest person to guard the frontiers of his country. Such suggestions and thoughts play an important part in the lives of all of us.

It is not possible to control the people and circumstances from where many of the suggestions emerge. Therefore, it becomes necessary to learn how to control personal receptivity to these suggestions, and the thoughts that arise from them. One should accept thoughts that enhance power positively, and reject the rest as useless. This, to begin with, may seem difficult or even impossible. However, it can be practised with a little effort. Just as in short fits of absent-mindedness one fails to receive a message, even though it might be conveyed directly, one can learn to deliberately close the gates of the mind, rejecting the suggestions when they appear to be negative and harmful. This way one can learn to screen all the thoughts finding their way into the mind.

To be able to benefit from the fact that positive thoughts enhance personal power and negative thoughts rob us of it, one must learn to differentiate the two. A thought is positive when it is useful in a given situation, and negative if it is not.

AUTOSUGGESTION

To take advantage of positive thoughts reaching the mind, we can practise what is popularly called autosuggestion. This needs to be properly understood. Each one of us is already practising autosuggestion. However, in most cases it is doing more harm than good. We are deliberately feeding our minds with suggestions and thoughts. Unfortunately, these are not positive thoughts, and therefore, we fail to derive any benefit from them. We keep wishing that we may have more power, but we do not back it with a firm belief in our ability.

To make autosuggestion provide you with a power that builds you, believe that you can become a more powerful person. You must believe that you are moving towards greater personal success. You must believe that you stand for all that is best in life — truth, honesty and thoughtfulness for others. When these strong beliefs penetrate deep within you through repeated positive suggestions, you will begin to experience the wonderful effect they have upon you. These little thoughts will transform into positive actions. These actions will, in turn, become habits that attract success towards you.

CONTROLLING EMOTIONS

When you learn to control your thoughts, you also learn to control your emotions. When we speak of emotions, we refer to our feelings of love, sympathy, kindness, fear, anger, hatred, envy, jealousy, etc. These emotions influence the prospects of success. Like thoughts, emotions also are either positive or negative. They influence a person's health, professional success, family life, and position in society.

Emotions influence a person's health and longevity. Positive emotions enhance individual skills and abilities, and also physical and emotional health. Negative emotions that emerge as feelings of disgust, revenge and hatred only contribute to keep one's wounds unhealed. One may succeed in belittling a person by giving vent to these negative emotions, but not without a significant detrimental effect upon personal power. Negative emotions rob energy and vital power. They disturb the balance of thinking and the physical functions of the body. The loss is still greater when one nurtures these negative emotions in the mind, and as a habit become a part of the personality.

One may not realise it, but emotions like worry envy, jealousy, hatred and a variety of fears are like invisible monsters that drain the system of vital energy and power. Significantly, most of these emotions are not based on reality, but only on imaginary thoughts. We worry about calamities that don't come. We harbour fears of things that do not exist. We are envious, jealous and hateful, without realising that we are harming none else other than our own self. The invisible monsters appear real only because we have allowed them to live in our mind. Each day they corrode into our character, health and life.

To make success your companion, you will need to get rid of these imaginary monsters from your mind. Write down on paper whatever worries you, or whatever fears that threaten you. Also note down what could be the worst that they could do to you. Analyse the problems, writing the pros and the cons, just as you would write the assets and the liabilities in a balance sheet. When you have the details of the problem on paper, it will immediately take the sting out of it. You will have clear facts before you. You will know where you stand. Even if the worst is imminent, surely worry cannot avert it. Fretting and fuming can only reduce your power to face the problem. Worry also reduces the power of reasoning. With the problem sorted out on paper before you, go ahead and put the solution into action. Look at the brighter side and ignore the dark one. You will have achieved reasonable results.

Positive emotions like kindness, love, compassion and thoughtfulness of others substantially add to one's power. Love yourself; love your family, your work, and the people around you. What you give of yourself to others will be added to you immediately. If somebody violates the faith you place in him or her, respond with forgiveness, which will only add to your strength. Hatred and revenge take it away. When the good effects of the positive emotions begin to accumulate, you will appreciate the power they can add to you. Your self-confidence will attain newer heights.

DEVELOPING SELF-CONFIDENCE

Millions of otherwise capable persons fail to succeed because of lack of self-confidence. Some fail because of their negative thoughts about their appearance and physique; others because of their family background. Many more fail because they are unable to forget a not-too-pleasant past. If a person must succeed, these insignificant thoughts must be overcome. With the control of thoughts, feelings and actions, one is able to adopt new useful habits. This way a new form of self-confidence begins to grow. A person then appreciates that he or she is no longer enslaved to sickly thoughts and feelings about the personal self.

It is necessary that a person must evaluate personal skills and abilities from time to time. This provides an opportunity to review both the achievements and failures, and improve upon past performances. Life is dynamic. Continuous change is a characteristic of life. Therefore, one must review the changes in the personality periodically to keep up to date. With effort, skills and abilities will grow, and also the self-confidence. One must concentrate more on the activities in which success has been achieved earlier. At the same time, one must keep learning new things. The added knowledge and the power that accompanies it helps strengthen the self-confidence. Try a hand at new activities. Success is the best confidence builder. Keep repeating your successes. At no time should your faith in your personal ability suffer. Increase your interests. Read books on new subjects. Join a club. Learn to sing, or play a musical instrument. Go out where you can meet new people and learn new things. With increasing confidence, your power too will grow.

Think it over...

Trust men and they will be true to you; treat them greatly and they will show themselves great.

— *Emerson*

PERSONAL CHARM

How do you rate your personal charm? Are you attractive? Do people give you a second glance when you enter a room? Are you content with your appearance?

Your physique? Health? The way you carry yourself? If you do not rate yourself very high, you cannot expect others to do so. Unless you believe in your ability to attract, you will attract nobody.

To be attractive, one must learn to understand the ways of nature. Nature has made everyone and everything beautiful. If we are not satisfied with what nature has made us, it is our own fault. We meddle with its ways even though its demands are few and simple. We must learn to step ahead with confidence.

Good health is necessary for a charming personality. To be physically fit, does not mean to have a special physique. It would rather mean that a person enjoys physical and emotional well-being. If nature has made you weak in a particular area, it should not be a cause to be discouraged. You should instead learn to live with these limitations. Nature has spared no pains to make the human body perfect. However, when we burden it with a load that is heavier than what the body can bear comfortably, stress affects the weaker areas, robbing the person of vitality. Therefore, learn to move at a pace that is in harmony with your health and ability.

To be healthy and attractive, the body requires its nutritive requirements to be fulfilled. The needs are varied. All of them must be provided to the body. Milk, fruits, nuts and vegetables are rich sources of the vital substances that affect the skin, hair, eyes, etc. They must form a good part of the daily diet.

The posture and carriage, too, enhance personal attractiveness. Good manners and a genial temperament also show. One is always attracted to a person who smiles effortlessly, and speaks convincingly. A person who has his back hunched, stands leaning against walls and furniture, and walks uneasily cannot expect to look attractive. In the same way, the way you sit, walk, greet and meet people will decide how attractive you are to them.

Clothes speak loudly of an individual. The way you dress can help draw immediate attention. However, one must remember that elegance of dress does not necessarily come from expensive clothes. Clean, crisp clothes worn without much fuss always enhance personal charm. Everybody appreciates simplicity.

It is said that the face is the index of the mind. It is always the centre of attraction. The main power of attraction comes from the thoughts. The greater the influence one has on the thoughts, the better are the chances of success. Just as happiness and gaiety attract goodwill and well-being, feelings of anxiety, worry, anger and envy leave their telltale marks on the face. So one must learn to be happy to be able to radiate the inner beauty of the self.

A HEALTHY BODY

Good health is a prerequisite to develop personal charm. The human body is a complex structure that depends upon many functions that must work in harmony to radiate good health and charm.

Every part of the body depends upon the digestive system for nourishment. The body requires a variety of nutrients to fulfil this requirement. If the food is varied enough to provide all the nutrients required by the body, there is no need for concern. However, since our habits and tastes make us drift away from what nature desires, problems arise. Many people are eating more than what they require. Others are eating the wrong kinds of food. This puts an unnecessary pressure on the body. The undigested food in the intestines releases toxins that make the organs sluggish. The body loses its buoyancy. Besides the nutrients, the food must provide sufficient roughage to keep the digestive tract in good condition. Fruits, vegetables and milk are necessary for every health-conscious person. Emotions have a significant influence upon the digestive system. This makes it necessary that one must eat in a calm and pleasant atmosphere.

Some form of exercise must be a part of the daily routine. Walking, swimming and various forms of physical work provide good exercise to keep a person trim. Exercise helps to increase one's breathing capacity. The deeper one breathes, more oxygen is available in the lungs for the blood to absorb and pass on to the tissues in the body. No shallow breather can look rosy and healthy. Therefore, learn to breathe deeply. If you cannot go for a morning walk, you could begin each day with deep breathing near the window of your bedroom. Your breathing capacity will increase gradually to keep you healthy and trim.

The skin wraps the body, helps maintain body temperature, provides a medium for excretion, and reflects the condition of your inner health. It can make you look sallow or attractive. The skin condition changes with age. Sebum, a fatty substance secreted by the cells on the skin surface, helps to keep the skin moist, elastic and healthy. During adolescence, the production of sebum may increase excessively clogging the skin pores. With advancing age, the production of sebum reduces, and the skin becomes dry, less elastic, and begins to wrinkle.

The colour of the skin depends upon the quantity of a pigment called melanin in it. The sun tans the skin. It can also cause sensitive skins to peel. The skin returns to its original colour if it is not exposed to the sun. In the event of an injury, the blood washes the wound and seals the area to form a clot. The healing process continues under the clot. Left alone, the injury soon heals, not leaving even a scar. If the injury is extensive, a scar may be left behind. Nature has a sure and effective method to protect you.

The skin is the index of inner health and helps radiate beauty and charm. Therefore, it deserves good care and protection.

> **Think it over...**
>
> Health is the soul that animates all the enjoyments of life, which fade and are tasteless without it.
>
> — *Sir W. Temple*

BODY CARE

A primary need of the body is to keep it clean. External care is much easier than the internal care of the body. One sweats more in the hot summer months than in other times of the year. But dust and pollution attacks it around the year, clogging the pores. This makes it necessary to keep it clean and clear. There is nothing better than a bath with plain soap and water to achieve it.

A bath should aim at keeping the body clean. The process of soaping and then rinsing with cold or warm water is stimulating, as it promotes better circulation of blood in the body. Massaging the body with oil before a bath also helps to promote better circulation of blood. This keeps the skin soft and supple. Very vigorous massage is best avoided. A body massage with oil may not be practical before every bath, but done occasionally, it is useful. For those who perspire profusely, particularly under the arms, an antiperspirant is useful. To ensure freedom from body odour typical in hot and humid weather, a deodorant provides the best solution.

PERSONAL GROOMING

A person desiring personal success cannot overlook the need for grooming. Men need not be as fastidious as women, but it is important that even men must take care to keep the hair combed, the teeth cleaned, the face shaved, and the nails trimmed. The general air of pleasantness reflects the personal sense of grooming. This is as important as the need for cleanliness. A man must shave everyday, have a manicure once a fortnight, or sooner if the need be, and have a haircut once a month. Proper grooming helps to enhance personal charm.

ETIQUETTE AND MANNERS

The bearing of an individual and the behaviour with others in day-to-day life conveys one's success consciousness. It can enhance, or mar, personal charm. The smile and expression on the face could either be inviting or repulsive. It reflects the level of self-confidence. Etiquette and good manners may seem trifling to many. To the person searching for success, they are as important as personal cleanliness or grooming. Etiquette and good manners reflect a person's upbringing, the education, and the ability to get along well with other people. In everyday life, adopt whatever that you find good. Take particular care to enhance your self-confidence that is visible in your personal bearing and dealings with others.

> **Think it over...**
>
> The making of friends, who are real friends, is the best token we have of a man's success in life.
>
> — *Edward E. Hale*

THE VOICE

The voice also helps reflect personal charm. Cultivate a pleasant and rhythmic voice. Have you noticed how a good speaker sways the audience with words and modulations of the voice? The speaker makes them laugh or cry. The audience sits still enamoured by the voice. No speaker was born that way. They learnt to speak to attract and hold the attention of the audience. This is possible only through training and personal effort. The latent abilities must be developed. To be a good conversationalist, take interest in the people around you. Make self-education a constant process. Stimulate your thinking through study, travelling, meeting and learning about people. The more knowledgeable you are, the better can you impress the people you talk to. Speak well of people. If you cannot, it is better not to speak at all. Unpleasant facts about others are best buried, rather than repeated.

MAGIC WORDS

Are there any magic words that can help a person project personal charm immediately? Yes, there are magic words that can do wonders for you just as they have done for all successful people. These words are taught to every child in school, but somehow, most people are shy to use them. When not used they are soon forgotten. These words are important to everyone who desires to make success a constant companion.

The first set of words is "thank you" or "*dhanyavad*" in Hindi. It is a simple expression of gratitude. Use these words as frequently as you possibly can. It would be preferable to overdo their use rather than under do. Use them at home with your wife, the children and also the domestic help. Use them at work with your seniors, the colleagues and even the subordinates. Do not forget to use them with the driver who opens the car door for you, the building guard who helps you carry a packet, or the liftman who takes you to your flat. Also thank the salesgirl who guides you to the correct counter, and the vegetable vendor who gives you an extra bag so that your vegetables are secure. You will be surprised at the response you get everywhere.

How does saying, "thank you" frequently affects the individual? It simply helps develop an attitude of gratitude in the mind. It makes a person grateful to his family, friends, and associates, and eventually to God, who is the source of both power and charm.

The second set of words is "I am sorry". Everybody is taught to apologise whenever one makes a mistake. But the lesson is soon forgotten. Unfortunately, even as a child when one becomes conscious of the ego, saying "sorry" appears to be a personal insult or defeat. Even when a child is compelled to say "sorry" he feels exploited and hurt. It is as though one gets crushed under the weight of the words, "I am sorry".

If you have to get ahead and make success a companion, you will have to rise above the others and apologise even if it hurts you. As you practise the use of these words, whenever you are at fault, you will no longer feel hurt. You have to use the words only when you are at fault. Sometimes there may be an occasion when you are not at fault, and only appear to be at fault, it is still worthwhile to say, "I am sorry" and get ahead in life. You will find that after you have apologised, your mind will always be at rest.

How does saying, "I am sorry" affects a person? It simply reminds you that you are human, that you can make mistakes. When you admit a mistake you mentally prepare yourself not to make the same mistake again. While on one hand saying "sorry" promotes humility, a quality admired by everyone, on the other hand, it takes away your pride, which could lead you to arrogance. It may not appear to be so, but this way, you are always a winner, a person well ahead on your way to perpetual success.

Think it over...

He enjoys much who is thankful for little; a grateful mind is both a great and a happy mind.

— *Secker*

CHARACTER

An important characteristic of all successful people is that they are dependable. This dependability is a reflection of their character. A person's character represents what he or she believes in. This belief can take a person to the height of glory and admiration, almost as though one were a God. When ignored, it can lead one to loneliness, failure and even ruin.

An individual's character is the most valuable possession. Its powers know no boundaries of colour, caste or creed. The financial status has no bearing on it either. The character is a potent power that when developed in its noblest form, knows no limitations. It easily overshadows the possession of riches, knowledge, intellect, or genius.

Great personal power can be developed through a noble character. To attain it, one needs to be dutiful, conscientious, truthful and honest. All religions also teach us the same thing. To convince a person the simple truth is written in many forms, and illustrated with lives of men and women who were perhaps no different from what we are.

When you accept the principles of truthfulness, honesty and thoughtfulness for others, and make them a part of you, you have a very vital force to attain success. It is a force that has identified all great men who became immortal through their thoughts and actions. This force can, as it has with all great people, extend the area of influence over a very large area.

Character is not reflected through a single act of great intelligence, genius, or greatness. It is made up of little day-to-day seemingly insignificant details of life. Every fleeting thought affects it. Thoughts become actions, and actions turn into habits. The laws of action and reaction hold well with everything we do. Only we may not understand it. No deed, good or bad, goes un-rewarded, or punished. Sometimes their effect becomes apparent at a later stage, but even if they are not, points are scored in your favour, or against you, immediately.

The development of character in its noblest form promises great rewards. The potential is unlimited. However, before it can be achieved, there will be hurdles to cross, many temptations to be avoided. There is nothing that a person cannot achieve with effort and determination. It will undoubtedly bring recognition and admiration. There will be a great power at your service. Success will become your constant companion.

Think it over...

There is not a man or a woman, however poor they may be, but have it in their power, by the grace of God, to leave behind them the grandest thing on earth, character; and their children might rise up after them and thank God that their mother was a pious woman, or their father a pious man.

— *N. Macleod*

POINTS TO PONDER

1. To succeed, you must take responsibility of your life.
2. Develop success consciousness.
3. You are what your habits have made you.
4. Thoughts are the foundations of habits and of change.
5. You can transform yourself by controlling your thoughts and beliefs.

6. Use autosuggestion to your advantage.
7. Emotions influence both health and longevity.
8. Lack of self-confidence can hold back a person from success.
9. Good health is a pre-requisite for a charming personality.
10. Cleanliness is next to godliness.
11. There is a partnership between good grooming and success.
12. Etiquette and manners reflect a person's upbringing.
13. Those who speak gently attract others.
14. Saying "thank you" and "I am sorry" can change your life.
15. An individual's character overshadows possession of riches, knowledge, intellect and genius.

Set Your Goals

Where are you headed for in life? Surprisingly, many young people do not know where they are going. If I were to say, "I am going", would you know where I am going? Of course, not! Unless I was to name or describe the destination, how would anyone know where I am going? If you have not decided where you are going, where do you hope to reach? A person whose object is to attain success cannot move ahead without definite goals to achieve.

When a person sets a goal, it means that he or she has an aim or a desired result to achieve. The person knows the object of desire. This means that the person knows what is to be attained. A person cannot shoot unless there is target to shoot at. If one were to just shoot in the air hoping that it will hit a bird, it might take the rest of one's life to attain success.

* * * * * * * * * *

A salesman was driving slowly through a small town when he suddenly saw several bull's eyes drawn on a wall. Fond of shooting himself, he stopped. On walking over to the drawn bull's eyes, he was deeply impressed with the shooting. The shooter had shot dead centre. Curious to know the person who had done such wonderful shooting, he asked a nearby shopkeeper who had done this great work.

“This is the work of the foolish fellow who lives around the corner”, the shopkeeper explained. He also guided the salesman where the person lived.

Still very curious, the salesman walked over to the house, and knocked at the door. A crazy looking young man opened the door.

“Does the person who has been shooting around the corner live here? I would like to meet him,” the salesman said.

“That’s my work,” the young man said with an air of pride. As a special favour he went on to say, “I can teach you to shoot like that in no time.”

“Really!” the salesman exclaimed. “How long will it take?”

“No time at all,” the young man boasted. “All I do is to first shoot, and then I draw the bull’s eye around the point I hit.”

* * * * * * * * * *

The story might be in lighter vein, but it conveys a definite message. There are many people who keep working without setting any goals, and if they succeed, they boast about it. Such successes are not based upon personal skills and abilities, but on sheer luck. A person who knows what he desires to achieve cannot afford to follow such methods. The person must get to know all about goals and goal setting. Without it, there can be no success. We must set goals because there is much at stake.

GOAL SETTING IN THE PAST

Are you new to the concept of goal setting, or can you recall setting goals earlier also? You might have been using some of the common methods for setting goals, but without being fully conscious about it.

You will recall that when you were in school, the teachers would spread out the syllabus over the teaching session so that they could cover the entire subject, and in the end, you could have some time to revise. Following a similar pattern, you might be spending a certain amount of time in doing the homework. You might also remember spending an equitable time on all subjects so that you may not lag behind in one of them. You might also have budgeted your time to create a balance between study time and recreation by way of games and other activities.

You will also recall that you might have followed a similar system in college, and in selecting a career. The patterns continue, only the priorities change from one stage of life to another.

You might notice that even within the family, there are goals to be attained. Every responsibility is really a goal that must be achieved if one is to be accepted as a responsible person. Each one of us has responsibilities towards our parents, the spouse, the children, relatives and friends. In different cases, the priorities may vary, but nonetheless, there are responsibilities to be fulfilled, and goals to be achieved.

An important goal that everyone desires to set is about life after retirement. Everyone is conscious about it, makes some efforts towards it, but many fail to attain what they desire. The principal cause for this is improper setting of the goal, and failure to define the various components that together make the goal.

Think it over...

Success is attainment of your definite chief aim without violating the rights of others.

— *Napoleon Hill*

THE IMPORTANCE OF SETTING GOALS

Most people agree that goals are important. However, they fail to set definite goals because they feel that what they desire is in their mind. It might be true, but it is not sufficient to have the goals in the mind. They cannot be translated to success unless they are clearly defined.

Have you ever seen an architect saying that he has the plans of the house of your dreams in his mind? We know he has it. But if the plans are to be implemented on the site, there will be the need for detailed drawings showing the layout of the rooms, the toilets and the kitchen. What will be the size and the design of the doors, windows, etc? In his drawings, he will also show where the furniture is to be placed for a fair flow of traffic within the house. He will also make drawings to show the path of wires supplying light or telephone connections, and also details of the plumbing. Many details go to make a home. All these details are worked out before the construction work starts.

How do you compare your life to a simple building? When such great details are worked out before building a home, can a person who desires success be satisfied by keeping the details loosely held in the mind? Can success be assured this way? Certainly not! If you desire success to be your constant companion, you will need to have the goals set in clear terms.

What happens when the goals are before you? For a moment, look back when you resolved to develop success consciousness in your life. You were especially asked to write down the resolution in black and white. When you set a firm goal you begin to attain it. The mind immediately sets a success mechanism into action. You begin to attract information and support to achieve the goal.

Let us try to understand this a little better. For instance, you are preparing to be a doctor and desire to migrate to another country. Then your goal will be to practise medicine in a foreign country. This will be your principal goal. Once you firm up on this goal, your mind sets working. It starts looking for answers to several obvious questions.

What countries can you possibly migrate to? You write down possible choices. The mind then asks what are the medical and health services like in these countries? You prepare a comparative chart. The next question is whether your medical qualifications are acceptable in these countries? If they are not, then what additional qualifications will you require? There will be many more questions that emerge from this goal. What are the living conditions like in these countries? Are there any racial or religious feelings that you may have to counter? Are jobs available in hospitals? Would it be better to work in a government hospital, or a private nursing home? What are the salaries offered to medical practitioners of your qualifications and experience? Will that suffice for you and your family to live there? Is residential accommodation easily available, or is it expensive? How much will it cost to commute? How soon will you be able to get a driving licence, and buy a car?

To answer these questions, you start collecting information and data from various sources. You are then able to draw conclusions, make further plans, look at finances, consult friends and gradually move towards your goal to migrate to another country. If you had not made a goal, and just kept it in the mind, you would not be able to progress at the pace you did. You would only grope in the dark wishing to be successful in your aim.

> **Think it over...**
>
> Have a purpose in life, and having, throw into your work such strength of mind and muscle as God has given you.
>
> — *Carlyle*

BASICS OF GOALS AND GOAL-SETTING

To derive the best benefit from goals, one must understand the basics of goals and goal setting. To be effective, a goal must be:

- Measurable
- Challenging
- Achievable
- Time-bound
- Shared

Let us take a look at each of these aspects of goals.

A goal must be **measurable**. If it cannot be measured then it cannot be a goal. It must be tangible and visible to be accepted as an achievement. When you decide to build a house, it is a measurable goal. The house is there for everyone to see. When you set a goal to be the Sales Manager of your company in five years, it is a measurable goal. You have something specific to show for your achievement. Therefore, when setting a goal, make sure that it is visibly clear what you set out to attain.

A goal must be **challenging**. A goal becomes challenging only when you decide to achieve more than what you are doing today. If you are a Sales Supervisor today, and your goal is simply: I will be a good Sales Supervisor, where is the challenge in your goal? Your aim should be to achieve more, and not only do better than what you are doing today. This is possible when you decide to place challenges before you. Just as one becomes a Sales Supervisor from being a Salesman, the next challenge before you should be to become the Sales Manager. You could further challenge yourself to become the Director, Sales. The greater the challenges before you, the more you will achieve. Success will follow you everywhere.

A goal must be **achievable**. It is good to aim high. However, if you set yourself targets that cannot be achieved under your circumstances, you will soon get discouraged, and rather than putting additional effort, you will tend to withdraw your efforts to rest in the comfort zone. There will be no progress thereafter. Do remember that the circumstances of every person are different. Therefore, the goals too will be different. For an average person it would be all right to have a goal of building a home. It may be an apartment, a cottage, or a bungalow. But if one sets the goal to build a palace, or buy an aeroplane, then one is bound to meet failure. These goals may be all right for a very prosperous person, but not for an average person. What is worst is that when you set out to build a palace, but end up building a bungalow, you do not experience fulfillment. You do not enjoy the glory and satisfaction of success.

A goal must be **time-bound**. If it is not time-bound, it does not serve the purpose of being an effective goal. Just imagine, playing a game of football without any time limit, or a game of cricket without limit of time. How do you decide who wins? It would be an utter chaos. When we set a time to attain something specific, we work harder to achieve it. We learn this lesson early in school when the target is to qualify in each class in one year. Similarly, in college, we qualify for a degree in a fixed amount of time. When people take longer, their names are excluded from the list of successful people.

A goal must be **shared**, particularly when several people are partners in it. This is particularly important when a goal involves the family members to attain it. For instance, if it is a family goal to move into a larger home in the next two years, the goal must be shared with all those who are involved with it. If the head of the family sets the goal without others knowing about it, and saves and collects money for the larger home, and if one of the family members rather than contributing towards the goal incurs unnecessary liabilities, it would be futile to set the goal. All the partners involved with the goal as contributors or beneficiaries must share the responsibility of the goal.

At the workplace, there will be many goals that involve several people. It is imperative that each team handling a particular goal must share not only the implementation of the goal, but must be equally involved when the goal is agreed upon, and planning done for its execution. If this is not done, there will be a lot of heartburn amongst those who are not fully involved. It will then become difficult to attain success.

WRITE THE GOALS

It is not sufficient to simply remember a goal. If you want to attain success, the goal must be written on paper. If more than one person is involved with a particular goal, each partner must have it written on paper. The detail of what is to be achieved, how it is to be done, and by whom, and within what time must all be noted down. When a goal is retained only in the memory, it is soon forgotten when newer thoughts fill the mind. This way, when more than one person is involved, one cannot be sure that everyone has the same thing in the mind. Besides, life is multifaceted. There will not be one or two goals to remember. There will be many pertaining to different aspects of life. The only way to ensure success is to have every goal written down. Why not buy an exercise book to record the many goals you will need to set in life? You could call it, "My Path to Success".

> **Think it over...**
>
> Providence has nothing good or high in store for one who does not resolutely aim at something high or good. – A purpose is the eternal condition of success.
>
> — *T.T. Munger*

GOALS AND FLEXIBILITY

Can goals be flexible? No. If a goal is flexible, it is not a goal. For example, in most examinations marks are scored on the basis of a perfect score of 100. This means that for every student, the goal is to score 100 marks. If most of the students score between 40 and 60, would it be fair to scale down the perfect score from 100 to 80 on the pretext of helping the students attain a higher percentage? The solution lies in training the students better, and not interfering with the goals. It is not necessary that the goal must be attained at the first try. One must keep trying. The more one practises, the better one performs. That is why you will see players practising everyday even though they play only on special occasions. The secret of attaining goals is to improve the skills and abilities, and not meddle with goals by making them flexible.

If flexibility is required, it is only in the methods employed to achieve the set goals. Sometimes, one does not attain the goal by conventional methods. In such cases, it becomes necessary to bring in some flexibility and employ different methods to achieve a particular goal.

LONG-TERM AND SHORT-TERM GOALS

A goal must be time bound. However, this does not mean that all goals must be completed in the same amount of time. There are some goals that can be attained at one sitting, some in a day, a week, a month, or even in a year. There are others that take longer. Therefore, in setting goals, one needs to remember that that there will be both long-term and short-term goals. They must be fixed accordingly.

For example, Sam Erickson was always fascinated by the position of a judge. He desired that he would become a judge in the High Court. Therefore, his long-term goal was to become a High Court judge. That is a top position in the judiciary. To reach it one will have to rise step by step from the lower positions to the highest. Since the position requires a high level of knowledge, integrity and dedication, he decided to set goals to personally gain the skills and abilities for the position through personal discipline, study and hard work.

The basic qualification required is a degree in law. His first career goal was to secure a degree in law with high marks and top position in the Law College. The next step was to gain some practical experience with a senior advocate. That became the next goal to achieve. For selection to the State Judiciary, it is necessary to qualify in the admission exam, and that became the next goal. After selection, the interview is the next step. To qualify in it was the next goal.

After training one progresses from the lower levels as a Civil Judge and Judicial Magistrate with limited responsibilities, to higher positions and more responsibilities. After a period of service, one becomes an Additional District Judge and finally the District and Sessions Judge, who heads the judiciary at the district level. The progress at each level is a goal to achieve. The rise from the position of a District and Sessions Judge to become a judge in the High Court is a matter of personal merit, integrity and hard work. This is the original long-term goal adopted by Sam Erickson.

When each step of the journey from a college student to a judge in the High Court is broken down into goals, each one taking a person to the higher position, we have a person having short-term goals, medium term goals and long-term goals stretching over several years. The greatest advantage of micro planning of the goals is that one knows where he or she is going presently, and what can be expected in a year from now, in five years and may be in ten or twenty years. As one progresses, it becomes necessary to remember that the skills and abilities have to be upgraded at each higher step. This way the goals are achieved, and success moves with the individual like a faithful companion.

ANNUAL, QUARTERLY AND MONTHLY GOALS

After a person has understood the concept of long-term and short-term goals, it becomes easier to understand the concept of annual, quarterly and monthly goals. If it were not for this concept, the world of business would never have made the progress it has made.

All companies adopt annual goals. Since a goal must be challenging, the annual goal is always higher than the achievement of the past year. The increased part is what offers the challenge. Since it would not be right to wait for a year to pass by before the results are tabulated, the goals are broken down as quarterly goals. That way, on review, if the level of achievement is lower than planned, corrective steps can be undertaken, and the goal achieved.

The quarterly goals are further broken into monthly goals. Sometimes the larger goals appear threatening because of their size, but when they are broken down as monthly goals they appear more achievable. A person works harder to achieve them. Besides, minor variations from one month to another can be adjusted to finally achieve the goals for a quarter. There always are seasonal variations, and with goals broken down, they can be better understood and attained.

Besides the business and commercial establishments, annual, quarterly and monthly goals are important to students in schools and colleges. They are equally important to those preparing to take up a career and those involved in the profession of selling. Business establishments selling consumer products follow selling goals aggressively. These are first fixed at company level, and then sub-divided to zonal, district and city levels. Goals are fixed for every wholesaler. What is noteworthy is that these goals are written down, and broken into smaller periods. This is the secret of the success of all good companies.

WEEKLY AND DAILY GOALS

Most people further break the monthly goals to weekly goals. Some of the top consumer products companies adopt and follow weekly goals. To them the sales made every week are important. They insist that every wholesaler must report the weekly sale. Deviations in weekly targets are taken seriously.

To ensure that the weekly goals are achieved, it is planned that a part of the goal is achieved each working day. Following a definite system of visiting customers everyday makes this possible. For example, the salesmen who sell consumer products are expected to visit at least forty retailers everyday. Cigarette salesmen visit as many as 60 to 80 retail vendors everyday. What is motivating each of these salesmen to follow the aggressive routine? It is none else, but the goals set before them. Goals are a great motivating force.

Every individual needs to understand the importance of goals. One must know how to adopt them, break them into long-term and short-term goals, and still further adapt them as annual, quarterly and monthly goals. Finally, these can be worked as weekly and daily goals. Every efficient person has a list of things to do every morning. The list is followed according to priorities and small successes achieved each day. These small successes pile up as weekly and monthly successes. Each year then becomes a year of success. The individual gets labelled as a successful person.

YOUR GOALS

We finally come to the most important part of goal setting – your goals! What kind of goals do you need to set as an individual? Many people do set goals, but unfortunately, these goals cover a limited aspect of their lives. Most people are guilty of restricting goal setting only to their career-related subjects. Other aspects of life are totally ignored.

Look back at what we discussed on an earlier occasion. It was agreed that a truly successful person is one who lives a balanced life, one who achieves success in every field of activity. When successes predominate in one field and are missing in the others, the development of the individual becomes lop-sided. The person cannot be said to be completely successful. Therefore, it becomes necessary to set goals in each of the following areas of life.

- Personal goals
- Family goals
- Career goals
- Community goals
- Retirement goals.

Think it over...

What are the aims, which are at the same time duties? – They are the perfecting of ourselves, and the happiness of others.

— *Kant*

PERSONAL GOALS

Personal goals pertain to your individual hopes and aspirations. Every individual begins life thinking of oneself, but gets entangled with the affairs of life to forget the hopes and aspirations. This causes a lot of frustration that leads to stress, sickness and low productivity. When the person finds fulfillment and is in harmony with the inner-self, one is not only at peace but also most creative and productive. Personal goals must be set in the following areas:

- Personal health.
- Education.
- Development of special skills and abilities.
- Etiquette and manners.
- Personal relationships.

Let us understand each in more detail.

When a person wants to succeed in life, **personal health** is most important. It is dependent upon the food one eats, exercise, stress levels, rest and the general environment one lives in. For good health, discipline is very important. With all the care it cannot be ignored that there will be setbacks that need special care.

The foundation of success is based upon a person's **education**. It is through the correct type of education that one develops **special skills and abilities**. Nobody is born with them. Just as it is important to acquire them to achieve success, it is equally important to upgrade these skills and abilities to keep up with growth in knowledge in every field. Everything is changing so rapidly that if one does not keep pace with the changes, one is soon left behind. Upgrading of knowledge is only possible through the daily newspapers, trade magazines and books on the subject. These must feature in the education goals.

With good health, education and special skills and abilities, it is equally important that a person must understand how to conduct oneself in the society. This will include the workplace and the community in general. This is possible only through developing **etiquette and good manners**. Many otherwise successful persons fail on this score because they do not heed attention to this vital part of life.

Personal relationships are another stumbling block for many persons. These people attain high qualifications, develop many skills and abilities, but never learn about maintaining good relationships with people. Because of this they fail to succeed, many times wondering whatever could have gone wrong when they put in their best? This aspect deserves special attention and must feature in the list of personal goals.

FAMILY GOALS

We may all be individuals in our own right but each one of us derives a purpose of life and strength from our families. The institution of the family is the oldest institution in the world. Wherever the structure of this institution is crumbling because of desire for personal and economic freedom, we notice rampant deterioration of the society. Many people are in need of and seeking psychiatric help. Family goals must be set in the following areas:

- The parents
- The spouse
- Children
- Dependent relatives
- Discipline and values within the home

Let us understand each in more detail.

We owe our birth and upbringing to our **parents**. In childhood, none of us quite understood the sacrifices our parents made to look after us, feed and clothe us, send us to school, carry us through bad health and sickness, impart values to us and more than anything else, to have prepared us for whatever we are today. Many mistake in thinking that they are superior because of their personal skills and abilities. The efforts might have been yours, but the parents built the foundation of your life. Many grumble that the parents could have done better. The truth is that they did what they thought was best. As a mark of gratitude, care and respect, one must form a part of an individual's goals pertaining to the parents.

An individual's family is founded when he or she marries. A marriage is not just a meeting and living together of a man and a woman. It has much deeper emotional bearings. The two together constitute a team. And like any other team, the team performs better than what either person could do independently. Both the husband and the wife have responsibilities towards each other. Setting of goals in this area of life aim at enriching the relationship with the **spouse**.

The **children** from the marriage further strengthen the family. It becomes the responsibility of the parents to give love, care and values to the children just as they received from their own parents. Unless everyone thinks in terms of fulfilling this responsibility, it is not possible to build a better world. As individuals, it is our responsibility to give it a little more than what we got.

Everybody is not burdened with the problem of **dependent relatives**. But when one has this problem, then one has to make appropriate provisions for the same. This means added responsibilities, and additional goals to be set to face the problem.

Nature functions on the basis of **discipline**. Night follows the day just as another day follows the night. Spring follows the winter, and summer follows spring. Then comes the rainy weather, the autumn and winter again. Year after year nature does not deviate. The laws of nature are eternal. They are based upon strict discipline. Successful families also follow a definite pattern of disciplined life. Each member respects the values and principles, which the family believes in. This is possible only when the family together sets goals for it to achieve.

Think it over...

High aims and lofty purposes are the wings of the soul aiding it to mount to heaven.

— *S. Spring*

CAREER GOALS

A little earlier, we discussed how Sam Erickson benefited from setting definite career goals. We saw how by setting goals at each step, he moved towards his long-term goal. It does not matter what career you take up. You may opt to become a doctor, an engineer or an actor, but when you set goals for yourself, you steadily move towards them attaining success for yourself. Career goals will need to be set in the following areas:

- Form of employment
- The position you desire
- The emoluments
- Updating skills and abilities
- Relationships with co-workers

Let us understand each area in more detail.

What form of employment do you desire? Some are happy doing a job where they are responsible for a particular area of work. But there are many who would not like to work under a "boss". They desire self-employment. They want to work at their own pace, and in their own style. Either way, the **form of employment** is a career goal. You must define the need clearly.

It is important to set long-term and short-term goals for **the position you desire**. With goals in place, success comes steadily. For a young Sam Erickson to set a goal of becoming a judge in the High Court may seem rather ambitious to many. But once a goal is set, one works towards it. One may aim to be a director in a company, or a brain surgeon, or even a space scientist. Some are happy training pets while some may desire to be a deep-sea diver.

People working at lower positions do not bargain about **emoluments** with their employers, but as individuals gain experience and expertise, it is common for individuals to discuss their requirements with the employers. This is particularly so with perks like a house, car, medical benefits, and an annual holiday for the family. Goals are often set to cover these areas.

To remain competitive, it is necessary to regularly **update one's skills and abilities**. Many companies have their own HR departments that provide training to the staff. Others hire specialists to conduct seminars for the employees. Some go for specialized training to institutions. Whatever be the kind of training, it is important to regularly update knowledge. Reading trade magazines and books on specialized subjects also help to update knowledge. This must be a part of the career goals adopted by a person.

All kinds of careers require human interaction. In some careers, one needs to build **relationships** with many people, but in others, the interaction is limited. Since people help to build or mar the image of an individual, it is important that this aspect must receive the attention when setting goals. It is possible to achieve success steadily when one enjoys good relationships with people who matter in your career.

COMMUNITY GOALS

Just as a person sets personal goals, family goals and career goals, one cannot afford to ignore the community. The quality of life depends not only upon what goes on in your family or at the workplace, but also in the community. Everyone seeks importance to enjoy self-esteem. This comes from serving the community in many ways. When one serves well, one receives recognition and importance. Community goals can be set in the following areas:

- Participation in residential area management activities
- Membership in clubs
- Contribution in religious activities
- Service activities in the community
- Holding elective positions

Now let us understand each area in greater detail.

It is a commonplace for the affairs of apartment buildings to be looked after by **management committees** who oversee the maintenance and security of the building on behalf of all the residents. Similarly, people living in colonies or groups of housing societies have management associations to sort out common problems. Membership in these committees fulfils the desire for importance and recognition. To develop such esteem, many people are willing to spare their time and effort. This calls for goal setting.

Membership in clubs also serves to develop self-esteem in individuals. Most people prefer to seek a membership in one club, but there are some who seek the membership of several clubs. After they have been members for some time, they further seek importance by becoming members of the management committees, slowly rising to the position of president. This is yet another area for goal setting.

Participation in **religious activities** leads individuals to seek positions in the management of religious organisations. All such organisations need dedicated persons who would help conduct such activities. The willing individuals soon get importance and respect. A few people serve several organisations to seek importance and respect through their hold on them.

Whenever individuals step forward to **serve their communities** in time of need, their efforts are always recognised. In return, they receive respect of the beneficiaries, thus fulfilling the need of self-esteem in the individuals. Many people serve in groups, others join NGOs to serve one community, or even several communities. All kinds of groups are serving the people. This form is a great source of personal success and happiness for a lot of people.

One of the most popular areas in this field is seeking and **holding elective offices**. People are willing to spend large sums of money to be elected to these offices. People in the villages seek to become members of the Village Panchayat. In the cities, they seek membership of the Municipal Councils or Corporations. Others seek membership in the state legislature, or even as members of the Parliament. Even within the political parties, there is competition for elective positions. Whatever it is, holding these positions does boost self-esteem. Many people who are politically inclined chart out detailed goals to achieve success in this field.

Think it over...

In great attempts it is glorious even to fail.

— *Longinus*

RETIREMENT GOALS

One spends the entire life with the hope that when he or she will be old and retires from work, then after settling the children, will live a quiet and peaceful life full of contentment and happiness. Unfortunately, very few achieve it for the simple reason that they did not have it in the long-term goals of their life. For most people, life after retirement from work is something they dread because of failing health, low financial resources, lack of self-esteem and an uncertain future. If one is blessed with a loving family, it eases the pain. Retirement goals must be set in the following areas:

- Place of residence
- Financial requirements
- Personal health
- Keeping you occupied
- Family relationships

Let us understand each area in greater detail.

Those who have built their own homes know where they will continue to **reside after retirement**. However, there are many who live in premises given to them by the government or other employers as a part of their service emoluments. Many feel that they would move in with their children if they are settled and working, but this is not always appreciated by the children, and can become a matter of concern. It is advisable to plan ahead for this eventuality.

Finances are an important consideration. After retirement, every individual is faced with the problem of a lower income. With people living longer and inflation cutting into the budget, the situation can become difficult for many people, particularly when they may have parted with their savings to the children. They expect that the children would understand and compensate them for whatever they have given, but it does not always happen that way. This can create undue financial embarrassment to the individual. Set definite goals to face this situation.

Health is yet another consideration to all elderly people. Most people are victims of stress during their working life. This results in poor health in later years. It becomes a matter of great concern with rising medical bills and lower income. Medical insurance looks partly after this situation, but it deserves the attention of every individual. One must plan ahead for it.

Idleness after retirement is a great curse. It becomes difficult for a person to **keep occupied** for eight hours, or more, that one was used to working. As they say, an idle mind is a devil's workshop. One is prone to think negative rather than positive. This lowers one's self-esteem. It is advisable to keep busy with one form of work, or another. Even part-time work would be useful. Hobbies too keep one involved. The important thing is to plan ahead to keep the mind occupied.

Family relationships can be a great source of strength, but equally so, a source of stress. Relationships change with circumstances. The children may not respond, as you may desire them to, because they are now adults in their own right. They may have a different way of looking at life. In such a situation, one needs to think and plan in advance through retirement goals that would necessarily be long-term goals.

REWARDS AND PUNISHMENT

How does one make the setting of goals meaningful? How does one ensure that they are followed? That they do not discourage a person when they are difficult to achieve?

The answers to these questions are within your mind. When you develop success consciousness, you always strive to achieve your goal. The secret lies in the level of your enthusiasm. And how do you ensure that your enthusiasm does not lag behind? Reward yourself for a positive goal achieved. Take time to indulge yourself. Take your family out to the cinema, or a meal. Buy yourself a small gift. This keeps reminding you of success. And what should you do if you fail to achieve the goal? Punish yourself by denying yourself of some goodies. Spare a few minutes in prayer seeking God's help to succeed.

POINTS TO PONDER

1. Unless you know where you are going, you can never reach there.
2. In every sphere of life, success comes from setting goals.
3. Goals must be clearly defined.
4. Understand the basics of goals and goal setting.
5. Goals must be written down.
6. Goals will necessarily be long-term and short-term goals.
7. Goals can be yearly, quarterly and monthly goals.
8. Goals can also be set for every week and for a day.
9. Cover every aspect of life when setting goals.
10. Reward and punish yourself for goals attained or missed.

Prepare a Plan of Action

We have just learnt how important it is to set goals in our life. It is equally important that the goals must be written down so that you can see them, think of them and strive to attain them. It was suggested that you keep a notebook to define the many forms of goals we discussed. Do not miss out on this exercise. It will spell the difference between success and failure.

Once you have the goals before you, you need to get down to work. You cannot wait for inspiration to stir you to activity. A certain amount of work must be done regularly. What is still more important, it must take you closer to your goal. Success cannot come out of haphazard work. You will need to formulate a definite plan of action for yourself. The plan must take into consideration your skills and abilities, and also your strengths and limitations. You must work with a singleness of purpose. The Plan of Action must define the time for work, and time for relaxation and leisure. You must strive for balanced growth.

For the many goals you set for yourself, you will need a certain amount of knowledge to achieve your objectives. If you possess the necessary knowledge, it is well and good. If you do not, then you may like to acquire it. There must be a provision for it in your Plan of Action. You may also need to build a library of information that you may require. This is important because not everything can be remembered. When one tries to fill the mind with information that may be required only occasionally, one may end up with a confused state of mind. Instead, it is preferable to learn how to maintain and get pertinent information whenever it may be required.

PERSONAL HEALTH GOALS

What goals have you set to ensure good health? Is the food you are eating all right? Is it nutritious? Or are you compromising nutrition for taste? Do you eat on time? Do you eat regularly, or occasionally miss a meal because of your work? Is the food well cooked? How often do you eat out?

Do you exercise regularly? Do you visit a gym? Or prefer to exercise at home? Or go for walking every morning, or evening? Do you prefer to jog in a nearby park? Or go for swim at the club pool? Many get their exercise at work when they work in a factory, or have outdoor responsibilities in the marketplace. What steps have you decided to take that you get adequate exercise everyday?

Do you live a stressful life? Or are you relaxed? Do you have a control over anger? Over your emotions? Do you get upset easily? Can you face criticism without losing your temper? Does any kind of defeat hurt you? How do you keep your stress under control? Does it reflect through physical problems like a headache or an upset stomach?

Are you able to sleep well? How many hours of sleep do you get? Is the sleep restful? Or do you remain restless throughout the night and get up feeling tired? What do you do to face such a situation? Do you rely upon a sleep-inducing drug? Or alcohol? Do you sometimes make up by sleeping late on a holiday? Or by taking a brief afternoon nap?

How often do you weigh yourself? What is your weight? Is it normal in proportion to your height? Are you underweight? Or overweight? Do you sometimes get your blood pressure checked? Is it normal? Are you prone to headaches, coughs and colds? How often do they occur? Have you tried to analyse if they are linked with the eating habits or your lifestyle? Do you sometimes get your urine and blood samples checked? Are they normal?

The answers to these questions will tell you a lot about your personal health. They will lead you to goals that need to be set to take you towards a successful life. From these goals, you will get action points. A Plan of Action to face the situation will then emerge.

Just as you resolved to develop success consciousness, you will need to develop health consciousness. This will ensure that you eat correctly, exercise every day, sleep well and avoid stressful situations.

Your Plan of Action could include some of these statements.

I will develop health consciousness. Action point: I will maintain a record of personal health. Whenever I go for a checkup, I will note the details in it.

I will keep a control over my weight. Action point: I must weigh myself once on the 15th of every month. I will record the date and weight in my health record.

Even if I stay well, I will visit my dentist and family doctor once every six months. Action point: I will visit them in January and July every year.

I must get a routine checkup of urine and blood samples once a year. Action point: I will do this in January every year.

I will exercise regularly. Action point: I will take a morning / evening walk. Or I will exercise everyday for half an hour at home.

I will keep my life free from stress. Action point: I will try to avoid situations that cause stress. To counter stress, I will have hobbies / will play outdoor games / do meditation / be in the company of positive people.

I must get adequate sleep. Action point: I will follow a set routine. I will go to bed in time, and wake up in time. I will not rely upon alcohol or drugs to relax. I will adopt a relaxed outlook of life.

EDUCATION GOALS

What education goals have you set up? Do you presently have the skills or abilities that are required for the long-term and short-term goals you have fixed for yourself? What steps are you taking to update your skills and abilities regularly? What newspapers or trade magazines do you read regularly? How many books do you read in a year? What are the subjects of the books you read? On the basis of these questions, you can set goals, and a Plan of Action will emerge from the goals.

I will update my skills and abilities regularly. Action point: I will subscribe to magazines "X" and "Y", and read them regularly. I will attend a training seminar in my field of work at least once every year.

I must read 12 books every year. Action point: I must buy one book every month, or join a lending library from where I can get a book on monthly basis. Four of these books will be career-oriented, two on personal development, and the rest for recreation purposes.

Think it over...

The purpose of all higher education is to make men aware of what was and what is; to incite them to probe into what may be. It seeks to teach them to understand, to evaluate, and to communicate.

— *Otto Klepner*

PERSONAL BEHAVIOUR GOALS

Are you satisfied with the way you conduct yourself in public? Are you hesitant to get into certain situations? How do you cope with them? What steps do you need to take to be comfortable in particular situations? On the basis of these questions, certain goals will need to be set, and then a Plan of Action will emerge from the goals.

I feel uncomfortable dealing with the opposite sex. Action point: To get over the fear I must get into these situations more often. I must take control over me and feed my mind with thoughts of confidence. I must smile and be patient in these situations.

I feel uneasy when I visit a family where someone has died. Action point: Take a deep breath, take control over you, and quietly wish the family by folding your hands together. Do not speak until you regain your bearings. Speak gently with concern.

Similarly, if you have problems dealing with individuals in different circumstances, you will need to set goals, and have a Plan of Action to attain these goals.

FAMILY GOALS

Are you satisfied with your parents? Or do you love one parent more than the other? Why? Do you have any childhood complaints you have not been able to get over? Did your parents build your life on a strong foundation? What values that they gave you are cherished by you? Do you disagree with some of the things they taught you? What are they? Why do you think they are unnecessary? What is the level of respect you have for your parents?

Are you married? If not, what kind of spouse would you desire? Why? If already married, have the two of you been able to adjust with each other? In what areas is adjustment lacking? What are you willing to do to bridge this gap? Do the two of you form a good team? Is the thinking of this team compatible with the thinking of your parents? Your family? Are there any points of disagreement? How do you plan to sort them out?

Do you have any children? How big a family do you desire? Do you feel that you have certain responsibilities towards the children? Are you and your spouse in agreement about the responsibilities each one of you fulfils? If not, why not? How can the situation be corrected? Are you making efforts to ensure that your children achieve more than you? Is your relationship with them founded upon deep emotional love and care?

Do you have any dependent relatives? What are their problems? How do you plan to cope with the situation?

Is your family life based upon discipline? Does everyone in the family understands and follows an unwritten code of behaviour? Does the family function as a team? Or does everyone follow his or her own line of action? Can you say that all of you are together in happiness, and at the time of a crisis? What steps do you have in mind to ensure happiness for the family?

When you answer the questions on various aspects of family goals, you will need to set several goals pertaining to each area, and on the basis of these goals develop a Plan of Action for you to follow. Some of the statements that emerge may be like these.

I owe a lot to my parents for what they have done for me. Action point: I will always respect and care for my parents. I will give priority to my relationship with them. I will expect the same from my spouse and our children.

My parents are self-sufficient and live away from me. Action point: I will keep in touch with them over the phone. I will visit them periodically, and will also invite them to my home.

My spouse and I come from different cultural backgrounds. Action point: I must put in extra effort to understand and respect my spouse's parents and family. I expect the same from my spouse.

My spouse and I work in different offices. Action point: I will respect my spouse's need for rest and privacy. We will together build our home. We will be committed to each other. We must have an understanding about our finances.

For childhood to be balanced, children need the love and care of both the parents. Action point: I will give quality time to my children. They will get priority over my other engagements.

I have a widowed aunt who is dependent upon me. Action point: She has been unfortunate to lose her husband at a young age. She provided me love and companionship in my childhood. I will care for her. I will expect my spouse to do the same.

A home is not a home without discipline. Action point: The family will mutually agree upon a code of behaviour. Everyone will fulfil his or her responsibilities. The family will together share successes and defeats.

> **Think it over...**
>
> There is a great man who makes everyone feel small. But the really great man is the man who makes every man feel great.
>
> — *G.K. Chesterton*

CAREER GOALS

What form of employment do you desire? Would you like to take up a job? Or would you prefer to be self-employed? What kind of a job do you want? If you desire to be self-employed, what kind of work would you like to do? Have you checked on the opportunities in the field? Are you confident about your choice of a career?

What position are you looking forward to in your job? What is the next higher position? What are the prospects of growth? What is the highest position? Are there possibilities of your changing jobs? Does the job carry sufficient financial returns for your efforts? Does it offer respect and position? Are the perks good? Are the emoluments in harmony with others fields?

Do I possess the necessary skills and abilities for the job? Are there opportunities for upgrading skills and abilities within the organisation? Does the company have arrangements with a HR company? Or would I need to take training through my personal effort? Would this be possible when working, or would I need to do it by taking leave?

Will I need to deal with many people in my job? Am I comfortable doing this? Or should I look for a job where I deal with fewer people? Can I improve my skills in dealing with people?

When you answer the questions on various aspects of career goals, you will need to set several goals pertaining to each area. On the basis of these goals, develop a Plan of Action for you to follow. Some of the statements that emerge may be like these.

The job is very promising. I must put in my best effort. Action point: I must find out what my employer expects from me. I will put in the effort to fulfil his expectations.

The job is a good starting point. However, it will not fulfil the goal I have in mind. Action point: I will put in my best effort in the job to gain the maximum experience that I can get to be able to move into a better job that requires this additional experience.

I want to be self-employed. I want to be a franchisee for a good product. Action point: Investigate what brand names are looking forward to enter your community? What are the products? What are the franchisee conditions? What are the short-term and long-terms prospects?

I want to establish a retail store. Action point: Where would you like to establish this store? What products will you retail? What are the prospects? What are the financial requirements? Do I have the necessary finance?

The emoluments offered by the prospective employer are not sufficient. Action point: Take up the job and put in the best effort to convince the employer that you deserve a higher salary. If he does not agree, you will understand why he cannot pay. When possible, change jobs.

The salary offered is moderate, but the company has an excellent HR department. Action point: Take up the job and avail of the training provided by the company. In the long-term, you will be well compensated through enhanced skills and abilities.

The company is not willing to train me for a higher position. Action point: Take leave and pursue higher training. This will prepare you with better skills and abilities, and the company will pay you a higher salary. Or you can change the job where your skills and abilities will be better utilized.

Dealing with too many people makes me uncomfortable. Action point: Take up a position, which requires analysis and research and not dealing with many people.

Think it over...

To be a success in business, be daring, be first and be different.

— *Anon*

COMMUNITY GOALS

What kind of recognition do you wish to seek in your community? Are you a member or office bearer in your housing society?

Are you a member of a club? What kind of a club is it? Social? Sports oriented? A service club? Are you well involved in its activities? Has this membership helped you network in the society? Are you holding any office in the management of the club? If not, what position would you like to hold? Can you think of improvements that need to be introduced in the working of the club?

Do you visit a place of prayer? A temple? A church? A mosque? Are you involved in the activities? Do you have a guru? Do you visit his ashram?

Are you a member of a NGO? Of any kind of service club? Do you volunteer your services for a public cause? Do you enjoy serving to a public cause? How involved are you in these activities? Do you enjoy them? Are you holding an office in any of these service organisations?

Do you belong to a political party? Are you actively involved? Do you hold an office in the party? At village level? Or city level? Or at state or central levels? Have you offered yourself for an elective office? Are you holding any such office? Do you enjoy holding the position?

When you answer the questions on various aspects of community goals, you will need to set several goals pertaining to each area, and on the basis of these goals develop a Plan of Action for you to follow. Some of the statements that emerge may be like these.

The apartment building I live in needs to be better maintained. Action point: Offer to become a member of the building society.

The roads in our colony need to be repaired. Action point: Call a meeting of the residents of the colony. Together make an application to the Municipal Council.

The club you belong to needs to expand its catering services. Action point: Offer to be elected to the Catering Committee of the club.

The Sports Club you belong to needs to be expanded. Action point: Express your views at the general meeting of the club; propose names of new members; help raise funds.

The temple you go to needs to be improved. Action point: Offer to contribute for the improvement; motivate others to help with funds and personal labour to improve the temple.

An eye relief camp is being organised in a nearby village. Action point: You offer your services as a volunteer.

The local school is proposing to build a new block. Action point: as an architect, you offer your services to design the building free of charge.

The elections of the state legislature are due in three months. Action point: As an active member of your political party, you offer to stand for the position.

Think it over...

If one advances confidently in the direction of his dreams, and endeavours to live the life, which he has imagined, he will meet with success unexpected in common hours.

— *Henry David Thoreau*

A PLAN OF ACTION

We have just seen how on the basis of the goals we have set, we can develop a Plan of Action. The discussion so far has been based on different goals, and how they can be acted upon. In any Plan of Action, you must write your goal – what you wish to attain. The next consideration is what steps you will have to take to attain the goal. You will also need to consider what support you can get from others to attain your goal. Do you anticipate any hurdles or obstacles? How exactly would you handle them? To succeed, it would be necessary to conduct periodic reviews of your activities, and if you lag behind, then how you can make up for it. In preparing your Plan of Action, there are some additional considerations. Let us discuss these also.

USE YOUR CREATIVE SKILLS

When you have goals in life to achieve, you need to search for ways and means to achieve them. One of the best sources of power, a source that can continuously supply you with ideas to explore new areas of success, is your own creative power. Everyone has it. Few know how to develop or use it. Once you have learnt how to use this wonderful power, it becomes a perpetual fountain of new ideas. This power will keep you going even when others have resigned themselves to defeat and failure.

Creativity grows with successful living. You can begin with successes in small things. Each success prepares for a yet bigger success. Learn to be happy, to be at ease, physically and emotionally. As one eliminates frustrating defeats and concentrates on areas of success, self-confidence grows, and creativity blossoms. All ideas begin as a little thought. Play around with it in the mind. Let imagination do its work. Analyse the ideas. Investigate their utility, and let them crystallize into a plan. Then execute the plans to become a reality. For a regular supply of creative thoughts, keep your subconscious mind busy. Use it to advantage as often as you can. It is like any other power. The more you use it, the better and more reliable it becomes. Use it to create opportunities for success, and to get ahead in life.

DARE TO BE DIFFERENT

If it had not been for people who dared to be different, we might still have been living in the Stone Age. All progress has come about because there were people who wanted to venture into the unknown. For their daring attitudes, these people were rewarded with public recognition and material benefits, both of them symbols of success.

The risk that a person takes in being different is always rewarded by success. The refusal to take the risk is an expression of lack of confidence to follow up one's thinking and goals with action. It is an expression of doubt about the ability to succeed. It is not suggested that one must plunge into action just because there can be no worthy success without a certain amount of risk. All risks are not the same. You must calculate your risks. Once you are satisfied that the odds are in your favour, do not let the fear of being different hold you back.

When you feel that changing your job to a more progressive company will bring you faster success, do go ahead. If you feel that it will be to your advantage to close down an age-old business and start another one, do go ahead. So is it with everything else. Try a new décor in your home. Offer a new type of service in your business. Plan a different kind of a programme at your club. Offer to do new kinds of things, and then prove that you can make a success of each of them.

ACT ON YOUR PLANS

There is no substitute for hard work. The setting of challenging goals, preparing a good Plan of Action, acquiring skills and abilities, and developing new and better ideas are wonderful ingredients to achieve success. However, none of them are useful unless they are implemented. What is required is hard work. There is need for honest action.

It does not matter whether you are a teacher, a manager, a salesman or a company director, to succeed you must fulfil the responsibilities attached to your position. Unless you work your way to the position you desire, you cannot succeed. Many people fall out of line to attain their ultimate goal at this stage. Despite possessing the skills and abilities required to be successful, they fail because they do not know how to put their plans into action. To a great extent, the fault lies in their personal attitudes. They lack sufficient confidence in their actions. They are afraid of criticism and defeat. In all likelihood, they have not been able to develop sufficient success consciousness in their minds. They are constantly weighed down by fears of various kinds.

If you are a victim of such fears, now is the time to change your outlook. Do analyse the strengths and weaknesses of your thoughts and ideas, but do not let indecision hold you back. To be a success, you must act.

You must implement your plans. You must plunge forward to attain your goals in life.

CONCENTRATION

With a goal before you, success follows when you make a serious effort to achieve what you set out to do. You must put in your best effort. Let nothing interrupt you. Let nothing reduce the force you apply to attain the goal you have before you. Why divide your attention and efforts on more than one target at one time? Do not allow other interests to interfere with your work. Concentrate on one thing at a time. This way you will remove all external influences from disturbing the flow of energy and productivity in the subconscious mind. You will be able to draw on the vast reservoir of information in a form that is useful to you. Solutions to some of the most difficult problems are easily found.

Think it over...

Success in life is a matter not so much of talent or opportunity as of concentration and perseverance.

— *Anon*

MAKE THE WORK ENJOYABLE

The vast majority of people hate to go to work. However, the person in search of success looks forward to work as a personal challenge. Whether the work is arduous or enjoyable is not an indication of the quality of the work. It depends upon the attitude of the person doing it. All work is the same. It is for you to accept it mentally as interesting, or as boring. When you like your work, it will not only be a source of great joy, but at the same time, you will also be able to do it efficiently, both quantitatively and qualitatively. There is no reason why you should not like work, particularly when you know that it will take you closer to your goals of life. When you enjoy what you do, your work will not be a source of fatigue or stress for you.

DON'T BE SATISFIED EASILY

Do not be easily satisfied with your work. Make each time better than the last. After all, with experience, should it not be that way? Even if you are self-employed, do not compromise with the quality of work. Your work must be the very best at all times, and under any circumstances. Do remember that there is always a better and a cheaper way of doing the work. If it were not so, the world would never have progressed.

When writing a letter, ask yourself if you have used the best paper, printed a neat and impressive letterhead, and written it without any errors and omissions? If you are managing a machine shop, are you certain that production cannot be raised, or wastage reduced? If you are running a general store, are you sure that you are rendering the best possible service to your customers? Whatever you might be doing, and despite all the success you might already have achieved, do remember that there is always a scope for making improvements in your work. Millions of rupees are given each year as incentives to workers, who suggest improvements to improve quality, and increase production and profits. You can achieve the same. Render a little more service than that you are paid for. The better the service you render, more of the rewards you get in the days to come.

DEFEAT AND FAILURE

It is a part of human nature to make mistakes. These mistakes, in turn, can cause a setback in achieving one's goals. This can be very discouraging. If everyone would understand and accept this simple fact, many more people would rise to attain success in their everyday life. Unfortunately, most people are unable to face these setbacks. They succumb to them and resign themselves to their bad luck.

If there were no hurdles and obstacles to overcome before one could be successful, no one would appreciate those who reach the top. We call a thing good because we can differentiate it from what is bad. In the same way, riches are more conspicuous after one has seen poverty. So it is with success. Those who have seen defeat, value success more. To climb upward towards success, it is natural to work against the gravitational force of defeat and failure.

A defeat is no more than a temporary setback. Failure is admitting that we have lost our chance of gaining what we had desired. It is the opposite of success. Once we admit it, it is the end. Surely, no man on his way up would like to give up easily. To be successful, be prepared for temporary setbacks. Anticipate temporary defeats. They are a part of the journey towards successful living. Do not let the setbacks discourage you? Instead, use every setback as a springboard to take a bigger leap into the onward journey. Look at it from a positive angle. Do not look at it as a loss, but as something that does not work.

The more the setbacks one has to face, the more one knows of things that do not work. This knowledge is what we call experience. It has to be gained by actually going through it. There is no other way.

Think it over...

It is good to fail now and again – you learn a lot more out of failure than you do out of success.

— *Ian Hunter*

POINTS TO PONDER

1. You need to get down to work to succeed in life.
2. Look at life as a whole. Fine-tune the goals to have a balanced life.
3. For every goal you adopt, prepare a plan to attain it.
4. Set specific goals pertaining to your health, education, personal behaviour, family, career and the community.
5. Prepare a detailed Plan of Action to attain every goal.
6. Use your creative skills to be innovative in your planning.
7. To be successful, dare to do things differently.
8. Follow up your plans with action and with hard work.
9. Stay focussed on what you do. Do not dissipate your energy.

10. Make your work enjoyable to avoid fatigue and stress.
11. Do not be easily satisfied. The sky is the limit.
12. Persevere till you attain success.
13. Do not let temporary defeat and failure discourage you.

The Unseen Hand of God

In the **Bhagwad Gita**, chapter 16, stanzas 10 to 16, it is said:

"Men and women, full of hypocrisy, pride and arrogance, and having an impure conduct, live in this world with insatiable desires. Devoted to a variety of activities that end only with death, they are given to enjoying sensuous pleasures. They believe that this is the greatest of joy, the ultimate happiness. With innumerable expectations, they give in to anger and lust. With sensuous enjoyment as their principal aim, they amass great wealth through unscrupulous means. They live with the thought. "I have earned much today. This will add on to my wealth. I will strive for more. My ambitions will carry me ahead. I have vanquished my enemy. I will vanquish others. I am powerful. I am the lord. I have supernatural powers. I am mighty and happy. I am wealthy and have a happy family. Who can be better than me? I will offer sacrifice to gods. I will give charity. I will enjoy life." Enveloped in delusion, and addicted to sensuous pleasures, these people are blinded by ignorance. They are like the devil, and end up in hell."

The foregoing paragraph is a literal translation of matter written more than 2,500 years ago. Does it sound relevant even today? It describes men and women whose success has taken them away from God.

In the very beginning, we discussed "What is success?" We agreed that success was related to earning money, amassing wealth, having a variety of possessions, enjoying special positions and having people think well of you. At every stage, it was also emphasized that the symbols of success had their limitations. Success in each field leads to special accomplishments. The pleasures of life pull individuals towards them. In ignorance, the majority gives in. This is a common phenomenon. We see it everyday everywhere. The people succeed, they rise in life, and then they fall, not to be heard of again. This has gone on since times immemorial. Mankind has lived in ignorance, just as it is described in the Bhagwad Gita.

Have men and women been so foolish not to recognise the pitfalls of success? When they learnt how to succeed and obtain the many symbols of success, did they not know of the limitations? What was missing in their Plan of Action?

THE MISSING ELEMENT

The missing element in the lives of people who failed to enjoy the fruits of their labour for long is "God". God has given everyone the choice of thinking and acting as each man or woman deem fit. It is through this choice that every person exerts personal superiority over others. When one succeeds, one thinks, "See, I have done it. I have attained what I desired. I have learnt how to succeed. I am superior to others." This is where the ego begins to overtake an individual. In ignorance, the person feels superior. Each day, with wrong repetitive thinking the person falls into the trap of the thoughts, and slides to a point of no return.

In the **Ramcharitmanas**, Ayodhya-kand, Doha 171, it is said:

Vashistha said: "Bharat, fate is very powerful and compelling. Profit and loss, life and death, fame and infamy – these are controlled by destiny."

Can anyone deny the validity of what the great sage Vashistha explained to his student, Bharat, Sri Ram's younger brother? None else could explain this valid truth in as few words as did Vashistha. It is as true today as it was when first written.

Ask any successful businessman. He will accept that sometimes despite a foolish choice he earned a profit. At other times, even after much thought and application, he made a loss.

Has anyone been able to control life and death? With all the advances made by the medical sciences, both life and death continue to be uncertain.

Fame and infamy are no different. We know of young unknown people becoming famous overnight. Equally so, great rulers and emperors have lost their prestige and honour in no time. The great sage, Vishvamitra fell to the wiles of Menaka. Ganga developed a relationship with Shantanu. How can we explain these events, and many more? Is it not the unseen hand of God?

* * * * * * * * * * *

When Emperor Alexander invaded India, he was once fascinated by the accomplishments of a saint, and said, "Swami, I want to take you with me."

The saint immediately refused. He said he could not leave his motherland. The Emperor lost his temper. He said, "Don't you know who I am? I have conquered the world. I have conquered your motherland. Who can fight against me? How dare you refuse? I can have you killed and cut into bits."

"You don't frighten me, sir," the saint said smilingly, "You boast so loudly, and yet I notice that you are a slave of my slave."

This infuriated the Emperor even more. He shouted, "What do you mean? How have you called me a slave of your slave?"

Unperturbed, the saint smiled and said, "Anger and the other emotions are my slaves. They are totally under my control. I am surprised how easily you have bowed like a slave to anger that is my slave."

Before the Emperor could respond to the saint, the saint was gone.

* * * * * * * * * *

If the Emperor could have taken the saint with him, it would have been "success" for him. Not accompanying the Emperor was "success" for the saint. What was the secret of this success? Was it the wise response by the saint? Or was it the unseen hand of God?

In the **Bhagwad Gita**, chapter 2, stanza 47, it is said:

"You have the right to work only, and not to the fruit that comes from it. Do not try that your actions must bear fruit. At the same time do not be attracted to inactivity."

Again, in the **Bhagwad Gita**, chapter 4, stanzas 7 and 8, it is said:

"Arjun, when righteousness declines and unrighteousness grows, I take birth to protect the virtuous and exterminate the evildoers. To establish righteousness, I take birth from age to age."

The above stanzas guide us to the necessity of doing work, to fulfilling our responsibilities, whatever the consequence. We can also appreciate that God favours the virtuous, and exterminates the sinful. This means that if we desire that the unseen hand of God must favour us then we must pursue success giving honesty and integrity the position they deserve in our life.

THE PATH TO SUCCESS

Somewhere along your journey to successful living, you will come to a point where the road forks into two distinct paths. On one side, there is the more rugged path, interspersed with obstacles, discouragement, and perhaps, even temporary defeat. However, you know that it definitely leads to your goal or destination. On the other side, there is the apparently smooth highway, which promises an easy journey, but it is not certain where it will lead you.

Do not be tempted into hurried decisions. The first road is that of honesty and integrity. It may appear rugged and difficult in the beginning. In the final analysis, it is the only sure path. The second road may appear to be swift and pleasant, and may promise swifter returns. However, in reality, it could lead one to shame and dishonour.

Temptations come in many strange garbs and ways to test honest people. Even one mistake may be too much. A person could be doomed for life. Never forsake the path of virtue. It may appear arduous and difficult, but it is the only path to real success. Your journey to success may take a longer time. Never compromise with your conscience, or your character. The two together are your greatest wealth. As a source of power, they are within you. They cannot be stolen. Only you can lose them at your own will. Few realise this when they give in to the temptation of quick material benefits. The loss in intangible forms is enormous. A person loses peace of mind, happiness, and a chance for real success forever.

Think it over...

I cannot believe that the purpose of life is merely to be happy. I think the purpose of life is to be useful, to be responsible, to be honourable, to be compassionate. It is, above all, to matter: to count, to stand for something, to have it made some difference that you lived at all."

– *Leo Rosten*

THE UNSEEN HAND OF GOD

Even the modern management gurus do not discount that we cannot ignore the unseen hand of God. With all the modern techniques, setting of goals, preparing a Plan of Action, and putting in the best of skills and hard work to attain our objectives, we cannot forecast which way the unseen hand of God will take us. It is estimated that while we can be successful 9 out of 10 times that we make a sincere effort, it is that 1 out of 10 times that creates an atmosphere of uncertainty. It is this single time that draws us to God to seek blessings.

* * * * * * * * * *

Dalip was to make a very important presentation in his office. He had worked hard to prepare the presentation, and desired that it be a success. He knew that when he made the presentation all eyes would be on him. He wanted to look good, and decided to wear his favourite shirt. In the morning, on the day of the presentation, when he came out of the bathroom and opened his cupboard to take out the shirt, much to his displeasure, the shirt was crushed. He called out to his wife, who came running. She could see that he was angry even though he had no reason to be because he preferred to look after his own wardrobe. As a gesture of cooperation, she immediately offered to iron it even though it meant some delay in serving the breakfast.

In the commotion over the ironing of the shirt, Dalip's daughter missed the school bus. To make up for lost time, Dalip refused to eat breakfast and drove his daughter to school before reaching his office ten minutes late. Looking at his watch, Dalip's boss expressed displeasure at his being late to office, particularly when he had to consult the boss before the presentation. By now Dalip was quite upset. Despite the best of skills and hard work, the presentation did not go off well. This only added to the displeasure of both Dalip and his boss.

* * * * * * * * * *

Unfortunately, what could have been a successful presentation failed to create the impact. Who should be blamed for this fiasco? Looking back, it can be said that if Dalip wanted to wear a particular shirt, he should have had it ready the night before. Or he could have got up a few minutes earlier that morning and checked up on his clothes. If he did neither of these things, he should still have remained calm, and not lost his temper on seeing the crumpled shirt. He could have worn another shirt. If he got late in reaching the office, he should still have remained calm. He should have realised that if he lost his temper, only he would suffer for it.

It seems obvious that Dalip was really to blame. If he had control over himself, he would have remained calm and composed. But where does the unseen hand of God come into this? It does. Dalip is an important and responsible executive in his office. This is not the first time he was working to succeed. He had attained many successes earlier, many of them much larger than the one he desired to attain through the presentation. What clouded his judgement on this occasion? What else but the unseen hand of God.

This is not the first time it happened to an individual. We have all experienced it. We see it happening everyday. In the Ramayan, we read of Kaikeyi, Sri Ram's favourite mother, asking Dasrath not to make Sri Ram the king, and send him to fourteen years of exile in a forest. And who was able to convince Kaikeyi to ask this of the King? None other than a crafty, hunchbacked maidservant, Manthra, who was able to change the destiny of the kingdom in less than a day.

In the Ramayan, we also read of Ravan, a very learned and capable administrator. Through his acts of learning and sacrifice, he had pleased both Brahma and Shiva, who had granted him very special boons. Yet in a fit of pride and arrogance he lost his mind to abduct Sita. This became the cause of his death. When learned and capable persons behave like Kaikeyi and Ravan, how else would we explain such errant behaviour except as the unseen hand of God?

We fail to recognise the unseen hand of God, and rather blame the individual for the lapses because God resides within each one of us. We fail to recognise Him because of our own ignorance.

> **Think it over...**
>
> Success is not fame, wealth or power; rather it is seeking, knowing, loving and obeying God. If you seek, you will know; if you know, you will love; if you love, you will obey.
>
> — *Charles Malik*

THE GOD WITHIN

Can you see your image in a mirror that is covered with dust? You cannot because the dust prevents the image from being reflected for you to see. In the same way, people fail to see the God within them because veils of ignorance cover the true reflection. Over several births, human beings have degenerated because of their ignorance, and are unable to see the God within.

The only way to remove the veils of ignorance and once again establish a connection with the God within is to become virtuous. The skills and abilities one develops through education and practical experience are useful to attain success in the material form of this world. These powers have a limited application. When a person seeks greater strength and confidence that comes from the connection with the God within, rather than be satisfied with the skills and abilities only, one needs to become virtuous. This is possible by inculcating positive qualities, and gradually getting rid of negative attributes. This is very much like your own strengths and limitations you analysed earlier.

BECOMING VIRTUOUS

Just as every individual has strengths and limitations, everyone's life is also dominated by both positive and negative influences. Good actions generate positive vibrations or influences, and doubtful actions generate negative influences. And how do we differentiate between the two? Good actions bring joy and happiness for everyone. Bad actions cause suffering. Once a person becomes conscious of the influence of both, one begins to appreciate the need to develop virtues, and do away with bad influences. This way one can attain goals with greater speed and efficiency.

What are the common virtues that we get to see in everyday life? Some of the common virtues are patience, tolerance, politeness, courtesy, kindness, friendliness, sincerity, love, truthfulness, honesty, moderation, flexibility, forgiveness, generosity, thoughtfulness, being charitable, benevolence, being merciful, humility, devotion, conscientiousness, purity, persistence and steadfastness.

Through virtues a person can develop positive vibrations. On the scale, love occupies the highest position. When one loves, there is respect, co-operation, compassion, generosity and benevolence. Patience leads to tolerance, serenity, silence and peacefulness. Simplicity and humility lead to self-respect and self-confidence. Good humour, laughter and cheerfulness lead to joy and happiness. Courage and wisdom come from knowledge. Truthfulness, honesty and integrity strengthen the character.

People often ask: Is honesty and truthfulness relevant in the present times? In the *Satyayug*, the golden age, everyone was honest and truthful. Nobody said that it was difficult to be honest and truthful. If these attributes appear difficult to adopt, it is because mankind has degenerated over the years. Before being dishonest with others, we are dishonest with ourselves. We lose more than the other person. When you remind yourself of the loss that awaits you if you are dishonest, honesty and truthfulness will not be difficult to accept and follow.

The state of being true is truth. Truthfulness adds great power to our lives. To begin with we must be true to ourselves. When it is said that one must be true with the self, it means that we must follow high moral values in our thoughts, words and actions. This promotes honesty, compassion and humility. When we are true with the self, we will be true to the family, the friends and with God.

THE POWER OF LOVE

The ability to love is an ability to spread happiness. Love is based upon the feeling of thoughtfulness for everyone. It is like becoming God. It is only God who can love everyone without any conditions. God loves both the good and the evil. The more one gives of love, the greater the happiness it generates. Many ask if it is not unfair for God to love both the good and the evil? Why would God differentiate between the two? All are His children. Like any father, God loves without distinction. We can understand why God loves the good. God loves the bad people to transform them into good people. It is only human to differentiate between the good and the evil. *A person must hate the sin, and not the sinner*. Bad actions must be denounced. Successful people encourage everyone to become good. So must you do the same?

Once a farmer owned a beautiful white horse. He was well trained, and not only the farmer, but also the whole village was proud of him. One day the horse ran away. The villagers confirmed that he was seen running away to the nearby forest. Two days went by and the horse did not return. Showing concern over the loss, the villagers came to the farmer and expressed their sympathies. In his simple wisdom, the farmer responded, "What can be done? Perhaps God wanted it that way."

Much to everyone's surprise the next day the horse returned, leading four wild horses to the stable. Everyone was envious of the farmer's good fortune. He now had five horses instead of one. They came to congratulate the farmer on his good luck. The farmer simply said, "Perhaps God wanted it that way."

A few days later, when the farmer's son was training one of the wild horses, he fell off the horse, and broke his leg. It needed to be plastered. He was asked to go on a long rest. Once again the villagers came to the farmer to express their concern over the son's accident. Again, the farmer responded, "Perhaps God wanted it that way."

Many days had gone by, but the farmer's son was still bed-ridden. The king's soldiers came to the village and informed that the enemy had invaded the kingdom, and they had to take away every young man in the village to fight the invaders. The farmer's son was unfit to go, and was left behind. The villagers knew that there were remote chances of the soldiers returning from the battle. The farmer simply said, "Perhaps God wanted it that way."

THE BOUQUET OF VIRTUES

Virtues are like flowers. They give of their fragrance to everyone. Patience is a simple virtue. Everyone appreciates a patient person. It is not easy to practise patience because it requires great self-control to accept the shortcomings of others. Next to patience is tolerance – the ability to accept things that one does not like. Those lacking these virtues think patience and tolerance are signs of weak people. In reality, it is only people with great strength and self-control who can practise these virtues. When you are patient, you will be peaceful. Peace has its foundation in patience and tolerance. When you are at peace, you radiate joy and happiness, both symbols of success.

Mercy is yet another great virtue. To be merciful means to give relief to those who are suffering. It is the ability to give of one's self. The merciful are forever giving in charity. They know no sorrow. They are happy themselves and make others happy. They desire nothing from others. Those who give and expect nothing in return are truly rich. Their fortunes are unlimited. Through mercy they create hope. They spread a positive attitude and happiness.

A virtue that is difficult to practise is forgiveness. This is the virtue one uses to face betrayal. It may be the loss of trust, of being cheated, or may be of just being ignored. The injury and the pain of being betrayed are always hurting. The immediate response is retaliation. The more difficult option is that of forgiveness. This requires one to rise above the ordinary. One needs to act magnanimously like God. While retaliation is a negative response, forgiveness is a positive way of coming out of an injured relationship.

Another virtue that is difficult to practise is to be committed. Be it in friendship, in marriage or in business, making a commitment is difficult. To be committed means to be sincere always. It means that you are caring, dependable and reliable. It means that you have the strength of loyalty, integrity and character. Commitment is putting the other person's interests above your own. It strengthens relationships. It promotes personal growth and goodwill. Making a commitment means the loss of freedom of thought and action to most people. When no promises are made there would be no promises that could be broken. However, without commitment, uncertainty reigns supreme all the time. This uncertainty can lead to failure and unhappiness.

Humility is yet another important virtue. It is the quality of being humble. To be humble means to not allow the feeling of self-importance to overcome you. One is humble when free from "I", "me" and "mine". This is possible when a person gets detached from material pleasures and possessiveness. Only then God comes to reside within the heart. The feeling of self-importance leads to seeking attention and respect. These, in turn, lead to pride and arrogance. In their presence, God does not shine within us. Through humility, we experience the divine radiance, peace and happiness. It is one of the most precious of human attributes. It raises the ordinary people to angelic form.

Ultimately, to be virtuous means to have high moral standards. It aims at becoming a good person. There is no limit to the good things one can learn and adopt in life. A good and virtuous person encourages others to be virtuous. Use patience as the first stepping-stone to becoming virtuous and successful.

SELF-TRANSFORMATION

How does one become more virtuous? How can one adopt the many virtues we discussed? Follow this simple system. Make a list of all the virtues you desire to inculcate in your life. Paste this list on your mirror. Dedicate each day for the practice of one virtue. For example, on day one, you decide to inculcate truthfulness. Talk about the virtue. Practise it at home, at work, and wherever you go. The second day, you could decide to practise tolerance. The third day you could practise humility. This way, over a month, you could practise and become conscious of thirty virtues.

In the alternative, you could adopt ten important virtues that you find attractive. Each day make special efforts to practise one virtue. Repeat the cycle. Do not underestimate the practice of these virtues. With positive thoughts, your personality will experience a remarkable change. Every night when you go to bed spend a few minutes to reflect on your activities during the day. What were you trying to attain? How much did you achieve? Were you able to be truthful and honest? Were you humble and kind? If you missed out on some occasion, ask yourself how or why did it happen? This will increase your consciousness about being virtuous.

COMMON FAULTS

Just as one can be virtuous by developing virtues in one's life, one can also be the home of faults that can take one towards corrupt practices, lewdness, vice and even sin. While virtues add to one's strengths to attain success, these common faults may bring temporary satisfaction and joy, but lead a person to vice, evil and sin, and ultimately, even to destruction.

What are these common faults? Giving in to anger is the leader amongst them. It comes suddenly. It is the characteristic of the weak. It emerges from an unrealistic feeling of self-importance, and from greed and unfulfilled desires. The person who gives in to anger suffers more than the person at whom it is directed. Anger can best be controlled through patience and tolerance.

Greed and jealousy are also common everyday faults in human beings. They emerge from a person's thoughts. To overcome them, one needs to learn to be contented. Whenever a desire raises its head, one should ask oneself what he or she can give in return for that desire to be fulfilled. The ideal situation is when it is fulfilled through hard work.

Everyone loves to be appreciated and praised. However, there is always the danger of this leading one to vanity, pride and eventually arrogance. These attributes can rob a person of the ability to succeed. Hypocrisy is yet another fault when a person tries to show off to be what one is not. These negative attributes can only be countered by humility. A humble person knows that only the unseen hand of God controls fame and infamy.

Hatred and revenge are attributes that need to be shunned. They may give the temporary feeling of satisfaction and joy, but lead one to failure. People may have reasons to keep these feelings alive, but it is like keeping ugly memories alive by touching the wound everyday. These feelings are best buried and covered with forgiveness. Only a strong and positive person who desires to make success a companion can do this.

Think it over...

Mahatma Gandhi's list of seven deadly sins: Wealth without work, pleasure without conscience, knowledge without character, business without morality, worship without sacrifice, and politics without principle.

SILENCE

Silence and peace are synonymous. It is the language to communicate with God. Silence is the stepping-stone to inner peace. When you enter the realm of silence and draw your thoughts within you, gradually you come in touch with God. Love emerges from your heart. You feel peaceful. Do not think of your body. Focus on your mind, and on your soul that resides between the eyes. Soon you begin to experience peace and positive power. This power of silence prepares you to understand the unseen hand of God. It prepares you for greater successes in life.

TIME

Time is God's gift to all mankind. Everyone is given a fixed time to live. It is for an individual to either put it to good use, or let it fritter away. Respect for time is a great virtue. Most people abuse time – their own, and also others' time. It is a limited commodity. God gives everyone a measured quantity – no more, no less! Once lost, time cannot return. It is a virtue to put time to best use. Respect time. Use it for personal development. Use it for positive activities. Respect other people's time. Use time to succeed.

CONNECTING WITH GOD

When a person connects with God, one connects with a very powerful source of energy that assures good health, success and happiness. God has made every soul in his own shape and nature. Like God, every individual soul too is a tiny spark of light. Like God, the soul is eternal. It has existed since God released it. It will continue to exist until it returns to become one with God.

In *Satyayug* and *Tretayug*, when the souls were pure they could experience their connection or oneness with God. The souls are unable to experience this joy because of the degeneration caused by the negative activities indulged in by individuals.

When one gets over the negative attributes in life, one begins to feel the peacefulness of God. A few minutes spent each morning and evening in prayer and meditation will make all the difference. When you feel the peace, you will begin to experience a great change within you. Your concentration will grow. You will experience the pleasure of connecting with a great power. You will begin to understand why you need to empty out greed, selfishness, anger and egoism from your mind. Instead, you need to fill it up with love, purity, compassion and thoughtfulness. In return, you will experience joy, peace and bliss. You will begin to understand the meaning of success in a much wider perspective.

When one begins to know and understand God, one begins to feel and recognise the God within. One begins to appreciate a virtuous life. The self-confidence grows. One develops faith in what is good and righteous. One begins to appreciate that when God is within, whoever can be against us? God loves everyone. We begin to do the same. Like a child, we behave like the father. Like God, we too begin to share our love.

* * * * * * * * * * *

A group of friends went to pick up another friend. The mother walked over with the daughter till the car, and was shocked to see how drunk the friends were. As the daughter got into the car, the mother said, "Dear, may God be with you. May He protect you?"

"The car is too full," the daughter responded, "If God has to come with us, He will have to sit in the boot."

A few hours later, news was received that the car had crashed so badly that it was difficult to tell what make it was. All the passengers had died. However, to the surprise of the police, no harm had come to the boot that was intact. There was a crate of eggs in the boot. Not one was broken!

* * * * * * * * * * *

THE POWER OF PRAYER

There are two ways of connecting with God. The first is to observe strict self-discipline and austerity. The second is to take your mind away from the surroundings, and taking your thoughts inwards, concentrate on God through prayer and meditation.

To seek the power of prayer, sit in a quiet place and think of God by whatever name and form that appeals to you. Sit erect and breathe deeply through the nose. Sitting erect is important because when energy is generated within the body, the energy can move through the body without obstruction. Think of the qualities God possesses. He is calm, patient, tolerant, peaceful and exudes bliss! Think of yourself as His child, as a part of Him, possessing all of the qualities God possesses. Thank Him for having you as His child, for giving His qualities to you. Express your faith in Him. Ask Him to lead you, to keep you away from harm. Ask Him to lead you from darkness to light.

When you take your thoughts away from what surrounds you, and connect with the great power that resides within you, you begin to feel the joy and happiness God bestows upon you. With regular prayer, greater devotion emerges in the mind. The devotion should be so strong that God is compelled to become visible to the individual.

THE STRANGE PARADOX

It is a strange paradox that while the circumstances compel individuals to set goals that lead to material achievement, prayer and devotion to God take an individual towards the path to spiritual growth. In general, people appreciate and applaud those who strive for material achievement, and laugh at those who speak of ethics, honesty and spiritual growth.

Why is it that a person can either seek material success or spiritual satisfaction? Why can one not have both? Material successes lead one to attachment with pleasure, and the evils that follow. On the other hand, spiritual satisfaction encourages detachment. The two oppose each other. How can one have both?

However, those who possess and use wealth as though they are trustees can create a reasonable balance between the two. The pleasure of the peace within is much greater than what material possessions can provide. Therefore, if one desires a well-balanced success in life, one will need to compromise situations to ensure that the attainment of goals does not overlook the need for ethics, honesty and integrity.

SIMPLICITY AND SINCERITY

Keeping the unseen hand of God in mind, when setting goals for life one will need to ensure that simplicity and sincerity are the guiding principles. To make this possible one should aim for the following:

- One must live a simple life, which others can emulate. The food and dress too must be simple.
- One must rise above oneself, and be thoughtful towards others in thought, word and deed. One must accept others as they are, and not as what one would want them to be.
- One must practise silence. This helps conserve mental and physical energy.
- Do not allow negative thoughts to control your life. Love must counter hatred. Joy must overcome sorrow. Purity must replace desire and lust.
- As the God's child, behave like Him. Make affirmations that like God you possess the qualities of patience, tolerance, care, love, mercy and compassion.

Think it over...

Whatever you do, do it with all that you have in you. If you are sleeping, sleep well. If you are playing, play well. If you are working, give the best that is in you, remembering that in the last analysis, the real satisfaction in life comes not from money and things, but from the realisation of a job well done.

— *Anon*

POINTS TO PONDER

1. It is not sufficient to develop skills and abilities only to attain success.
2. God is the missing element in the lives of people who fail to enjoy the fruits of their labour.
3. On the path to success, choose the path that is certain, rather than the path that is easy.
4. Our skills and abilities help us to attain success, only 9 out of 10 times.
5. Success eludes us the tenth time because of the unseen hand of God.
6. God resides within everyone. We cannot see or feel Him because of our own ignorance.
7. To see and feel the God within, one must become virtuous.
8. Of all the virtues, the love for mankind enjoys the highest position.
9. You can transform yourself by adopting as many virtues as possible.
10. To add to your strength, get rid of as many faults as you can.
11. Silence is the language we use to converse with God.
12. Respect time – your own, and that of others.
13. Connect with God through prayer.
14. Live a life dominated by simplicity and sincerity.

At The Top

When a person attains success, one begins to appreciate the need for personal discipline, the need for goals, a good Plan of Action, and the many little efforts that contribute to help reach the destination. One also learns what can be positively helpful, and what cannot be. Since repetition of actions help build habits, success that is attained in one field can be achieved in other fields also through similar actions. Gradually, attaining success becomes a habit.

Success must never be enjoyed alone. One must share it with the family, the friends and colleagues. In due time, one must also share success with the community.

Success brings with it a new kind of confidence. A person begins to feel the possession of a new power with great potentialities. When this power is used for the welfare of mankind, it continues to grow. However, when used only to satisfy selfish ends, it begins to diminish. The negative thoughts and influences react on it. Used intelligently, it can help you to attain success again, and again.

THE JOURNEY UPWARDS

A person climbs up the ladder to success step by step. The journey upwards can be compared with a pyramid. The large base is representative of the big crowd waiting to go up. Everyone is in search of success, and desires to go as high as possible. However, each person settles down at a level that is in harmony with one's personal skills and abilities. *An established rule is that one attains the height one is capable of.* Even if one were to be catapulted to a greater height because of special circumstances, one settles down at a height that one rightly deserves. At each level, as one goes up, the number of people get reduced. There is place for only one person at the top.

The attainment of success is a source of great joy and happiness. However, this feeling of elation is short-lived. One desires to go up further, but when personal inability to rise any further restricts further growth, one begins to get frustrated. It requires continued effort even to maintain the height a person has attained. It is work, more work, and still more work. Since this work becomes the benchmark for the success, the person finds it difficult to withdraw from it. At the same time, with every effort going in to keep working, one begins to wonder what is the personal gain from success.

Since money is the most conspicuous symbol of success, most of the effort that is put in is in the workplace where money is generated. To attain this, other fields like the family and the society get ignored, creating an imbalance in life. With this imbalance, the worst affected is the individual because to keep up with others, one tends to ignore the self most, hoping to make up for it later when the circumstances are more comfortable. Even when one is conscious of the need for maintaining a balance in life, personal freedom has still to be sacrificed very often at great cost to the individual. Several problems restrict individual freedom and fulfillment, sometimes making it a frustrating experience.

> **Think it over...**
>
> Excellence is an art won by training and habituation. We do not act rightly because we have virtue or excellence, but we rather have those because we have acted rightly. We are what we repeatedly do. Excellence, then, is not an act but a habit.
>
> — *Aristotle*

FACING CRITICISM

One needs to understand that a factor that leads to great discouragement is criticism. Whoever attains success must face criticism. The most successful people are also the most criticised ones.

It is natural for the limelight to fall upon the people who make success a constant companion. From the viewer's angle, even the small shortcomings appear rather magnified. Therefore, criticism is likely to be exaggerated.

Two kinds of people inhabit this world. Those who work hard to achieve success. And those who try to bring others down with criticism. This gives them an inner satisfaction that they are no less important. These people never work sincerely, nor are they enthusiastic. They have no interest in attaining success. They take pride in tearing other people apart with criticism. It makes them happy to pull others down in public estimation.

Severe criticism can be a major discouragement in the path to success. However, when there are goals in life to be attained, one must face it with patience. It should not discourage a person from moving towards the goals. One cannot stop a person from expressing his or her views. But one can certainly control one's reactions to these views.

Use criticism as a tool to grow. Whenever criticism is hurled at you, check for any gaps or loopholes that you may have inadvertently overlooked. If you find that there is nothing to worry about, then take criticism as an expression of jealousy, and strive harder to achieve still greater successes. This way you will learn to be more meticulous in everything you do. Accepting that nobody is perfect, do not let criticism of little failings upset you. It is just a part of being successful in life.

MONOTONY AND LONELINESS

Other problems that can accompany success are monotony and loneliness. It is commonplace for monotony from doing repetitive work to set in. A person feels bored and loses enthusiasm for work. It can rob one of vital efficiency, and distract from the vital goals. An obvious remedy lies in working alternatively at different kinds of work. Try to make the work interesting. Keep yourself in a high level of motivation and enthusiasm. When you take interest in your work, you will find it interesting.

Few people succeed in keeping them in a high state of motivation. Therefore, at every stage, there are many dropouts. Only about five percent make it to the mark. The journey to success becomes a lonely one. There will be times when you will experience a great sense of loneliness, sometimes even to the extent of desperation. Not many people are endowed with the virtue of perseverance to attain their goals. If you do not want to meet their end, you will have to find a satisfactory solution to this problem. Your greatest support at such times can be your undying enthusiasm. If you can keep motivating yourself with thoughts of the ultimate rewards of success, you will have a powerful force preventing you from falling into the clutches of loneliness.

> **Think it over...**
>
> Only God can form and paint a flower, but any foolish child can pull it to pieces.
>
> — *J.M. Gibson*

PROCRASTINATION

To procrastinate means to delay or postpone action. This may be because of lack of confidence, some hesitation or indecision. The important thing is that there is no action. Without action, there can be no success. With some people, procrastination becomes a habit. It may not appear to cause any harm immediately. However, ultimately procrastination can seriously affect progress. It affects the day-to-day work, and ends up as a nasty habit, which can permanently affect the prospects of success in the future.

OVER-CONFIDENCE

Over-confidence is just as bad as lack of self-confidence. We may overestimate our progress because of over-confidence. Over-enthusiasm and intense eagerness to attain success can disillusion us to believe that we are making greater progress than what may be the reality. This may be harmless, but it can be misguiding. Over-confidence makes a person complacent. This may keep him or her away from success. It is important that we must take a realistic view of our activities and progress. We may sometimes feel discouraged at our slow progress. However, we do know that we are on our way to success.

FATIGUE AND STRESS

When one works consistently, it is natural for fatigue to set in. Fatigue can be due to physical reasons, or it could be due to emotional stress. Fatigue due to physical causes comes from excessive physical exertion. One can recognise it immediately when the body demands rest and sleep. Physical fatigue can be easily relieved through rest, relaxation and a good night's sleep.

Emotional stress, which is induced by the emotions, is controlled by the mind. Without the least bit of physical exertion, one can be emotionally stressed. It brings with it physical fatigue, and an irritable and moody temperament. Wrong mental attitudes towards life are principally responsible for this problem. Doing repetitive work and the monotony ensuing from it can also cause emotional stress. Very few people are able to cope up with stress intelligently. It leads people from one thing to another, but rarely are they able to rid themselves of it completely.

Many people resort to alcohol and a variety of drugs to control this stress. Neither of these should be used. Both are addictive, and lead to newer problems. Sometimes, as an immediate measure, a drug recommended by a medical practitioner may be used. The relief may only be temporary. Long-term treatment consists in adopting positive personal attitudes. This cannot be achieved overnight. It depends upon gradually changing one's habits. It requires effort, but can be done. One would do well to organize an interesting daily routine. Learn to enjoy your work. Do things that give personal satisfaction. Develop a friendly attitude towards people. *Learn to live and let live.*

Dealing with people can be a major cause of anxiety, fatigue and stress. Some people are insensitive to this kind of stress, but most people find the initial contact with people stimulating, but soon the stress begins to build up. The reactions of different people vary. One must make adjustments to find satisfaction from their relationships with people. It is useless to fret and fume to cope with this form of stress. The solution lies in a positive attitude towards people. There are no perfect people. We are not perfect. We cannot expect others to be so. We must accept people as they are, and not as what we want them to be. We need to understand why people behave as they do. What motivates them to their good and bad actions? Can this knowledge be useful to us? You will do well to remember that:

- Fatigue and stress should not be allowed to set in.
- Excessive physical strain and emotional stress must be avoided.
- Excessive noise, movement and oppressive weather cause fatigue.
- One should not speak more than is necessary. It can cause fatigue.

- Situations of conflict must be avoided. They cause emotional stress.
- Physical exercise, deep breathing and meditation help relieve stress.

LIVING A BALANCED LIFE

Many people succeed in life, yet there are very few who are able to create a fair balance of success in the different areas of life. Many great men and women who accomplished notable success in a particular field have failed on this score. Once in the race to succeed, most people get so obsessed by it that they forget the purpose of getting into it. Success should not be restricted only to the realisation of certain goals in life. It should also aim at having a happy home and family. It should also mean enjoying a position in the society. If success is lopsided and lacks balance in different areas, it would be of little value. It might give some psychological contentment of having achieved what one set out to do. A frustrated family is a high price to pay for personal success.

A fair balance between personal happiness, work, the home and family, and the society is the only solution to this problem. This way one can enjoy material benefits at the workplace, a contented family in the home, and honour and prestige in the society. One is useless without the others. Be fair to all concerned, including yourself.

Those who are in a hurry to climb the ladder of success sometimes consider the demands of a family as unreasonable. However, it is not so. Spending quality time with the family is important. It provides the bread-earner an opportunity to relax and prepare for still greater achievements in life. A happy home is a place to recharge oneself for success. Taking care of the community or the society helps build self-esteem.

To remain successful, you must promote yourself, take good decisions and strive to be efficient always. Let us discuss these in a little more detail.

> **Think it over...**
>
> Let your life lightly dance on the edges of time like dew on the tip of a leaf.
>
> — *Rabindranath Tagore*

PROMOTE YOURSELF

Good public relations are becoming an important part of life. Earlier, only film stars used to employ professionals to look after their public relation needs. Today political parties, corporate bodies, service organisations and business and professional people are giving special emphasis to good public relations, which is definitely better than advertising campaigns.

In the modern times, it is not sufficient to be a good worker and do your duty well. You will need to ensure that the people who matter know about your skills and abilities, and how you have learnt the art of success. This does not mean that you should boast about your good work. That would only be counter-productive. If you do this, rather than appreciate your work, you may only fall in their estimation. What is necessary is that you should not be publicity-shy. At the next business meeting, do not take a rear seat. Sit where people can see you. When asked, offer your candid opinions. Do not hesitate to suggest new ideas, or improvements that can be introduced at the workplace.

If you need to bring a problem to the notice of your immediate superior, clearly state your own inferences and possible solutions. The chances are that one of the solutions suggested by you may be accepted. This enhances your boss's opinion about you. Similarly, if you are asked to report about a particular problem, do not be contented by getting together the desired information. You will do well to supplement the information with ideas to solve the problem.

If you have a positive idea about the improvement of civic services, or about the organization and clubs you belong to, do not hesitate to propose your idea to others. Pass the idea to the appropriate authorities. Tell them how benefits can accrue from your suggestions. This way you can gradually build a good public opinion about your efforts to improve the society.

Do not be contented with the amount of work you are presently doing as a part of your normal duties. Do a little more than what is expected of you. This way, you are letting it known that you are capable of handling more responsibility than what you are doing. The little extra will keep you ahead of competition. It will also help promote creativity and make your efforts more productive. Each rise in position does not entail a sudden increase in responsibility. The little extra effort will automatically prepare you for the next higher position. Success will continue to be your companion.

MAKING DECISIONS

When you succeed, your responsibilities will increase. An important responsibility in all high positions is to take decisions. These decisions can take you to newer heights of success. However, if the decisions are not based upon correct understanding of facts and the situation, they can also lead to failure. To avoid failure, most people refuse to make a decision. They do not realise that not to take a decision is also a decision, and definitely a wrong one.

Decision-making is not as difficult as most people imagine it to be. One learns it through experience. Men and women who have learnt the art of decision-making are amongst the highest paid and most respected people in the world.

When taking a decision there are fifty percent chances that you are right, and fifty percent that you are not. However, if you avoid taking the decision altogether, the chances are that you will always be wrong. At the same time, you will unconsciously be developing the nasty habit of indecision. This can be a big obstacle in attaining success later. Indecision is a negative decision. It is the hallmark of the inefficient and the irresponsible.

Follow this simple procedure to take decisions. Note the details on paper until you can learn to do it swiftly in your mind:

- Define the problem in specific terms.
- Collect facts from all possible sources. Make allowances for any bias.
- Consider the pros and cons from every angle patiently.
- Do not let anyone force you to a decision.
- Take an appropriate decision.

You will do well to remember that nobody can take a correct decision every time. You may be sixty percent right to begin with. Gradually, your performance will improve with experience. A stage will come when you will always be right. When you do make a mistake, accept it gracefully. Do not rationalize it.

LIVING EFFICIENTLY

Success and efficiency are linked. To be successful, one needs to be efficient. When you are successful, you cannot afford to neglect efficiency. The purpose of learning to be successful is to live efficiently.

Successful people appear to be living almost effortlessly. After a full day's work, they still appear fresh. They do not show the slightest signs of boredom or fatigue. They are ready to provide satisfying quality time to the family. They have time for extra-curricular activities, and yet some more to participate in social life. These people find happiness in everything that they do. Their secret is rather simple – they are just plain efficient.

To be efficient means to be competitive. It also means to be able to achieve more in less time, or with lesser effort. It is to be able to do it without any strain on personal health or leisure. It means to find contentment and happiness in everything one needs to do.

INCREASING PERSONAL EFFICIENCY

Everyone is capable of increasing one's efficiency manifold. This can be done in two ways.

1. By learning to use the wonderful power gifted to us by nature.
2. By ensuring that none of this power is wasted through wrong and unnecessary actions.

Nature has endowed everyone with the power to be efficient. Unfortunately, only a few people can recognize it, or put it to good use.

The first step to increase personal efficiency is to become conscious of this vital force within you. It can transform you into a new person. The next step is to ensure that one enjoys good health. You must learn to be healthy if you want to be efficient. Even if not blessed with perfect health, you can still make the best of it by learning to live with your limitations. It is your attitude that will take you a long way towards more efficient living.

The next step towards greater efficiency is to carry out self-evaluation of your activities. Is your routine well planned? Is it free from petty annoyances, allowing you to concentrate on your main objectives? Is your time well utilized? Are you able to reasonably achieve the targets for the day? Alternatively, is it that you do no advance planning at all? You rely only upon an alibi each time you are faced by failure? The answers to these simple questions can provide a lot of food for thought. You can use the knowledge to increase your productivity in everyday life.

To be efficient, you will need to draw strength from self-discipline. Learn to control your emotions. Do not waste your energy on negative emotions like anger, jealousy, hatred or revenge. Instead, develop a wider and more positive attitude towards life. Speak less. A lot of energy is wasted on unnecessary speech. *Make self-education a continuous process.* Be on the lookout for improvements you can adopt in your life. This will gradually reinforce your self-confidence and your system will readily release more energy to be put to use.

Do not permit the obstacles to discourage you. They are a part of everyday life. Anxiety and worry can sap large amounts of energy. They leave one confused, tired and inefficient to tackle further work. Learn to accept defeat just as one would welcome success. This way a lot of energy can be conserved rather than be wasted. There is no one without his or her share of problems. The efficient person knows that there is a solution to every problem. The solution can always be found provided one looks for it eagerly. Nobody is defeated unless one gives in and makes the information public. Never let go. Persevere. Perseverance leads to success and adds to one's self-confidence.

Fatigue and stress affect personal efficiency in a large majority of people. We have discussed this problem already. To avoid fatigue intersperse different kinds of work. If you are overworked take rest. Try to understand the pattern of fatigue you tend to suffer from, and avoid causes that promote it. You may not be able to pinpoint the exact causes immediately, but as you become conscious of the problem, you can eliminate them one by one. As a rule, have an interesting working schedule with brief periods of rest. Balance work and pleasure in the daily routine. Do not overlook the need for good sleep. It is nature's way of giving you renewed strength for meeting the challenge of yet another day.

ORGANISE FOR EFFICIENT LIVING

To ensure that success is your constant companion, you will need to organize a plan for efficient living. This plan must touch every aspect of your life. Your energy must be utilized productively, bringing in more successes.

Your home is your nest – a retreat from the glares and the problems of the outside world. A home is where you recharge yourself for facing the challenges of yet another day. It is your springboard to greater achievements and recognition at the workplace and in society. You must seek the co-operation of your spouse and family. Harmony in the home prepares a person for great successes in the outside world.

We have already seen how important it is to plan. Plan all your activities. Plan for the next few months, for the weeks to come, and for the day, you are setting out for in the morning. Work out priorities. Fix time by which each task must be done. Initially, you may not be able to forecast your schedule very accurately. Some changes may become necessary. With growing experience, you will realise the advantage of working to a system.

Time management is very important if you want to be efficient and competitive. Allocate a time for all your activities. At the workplace, you must have time to read the correspondence, dictate letters, confer with the subordinates, meet visitors, work out improvements, confer with seniors, and for other such matters that require your attention everyday. Do have some flexibility in the schedule to allow you to attend to pressing needs sometimes. This way you will be able to handle emergencies without disturbing the normal work.

At the workplace, do not let interruptions distract you. Tackle one issue at a time. If you were to take up several things simultaneously, everything would end up in confusion. This could sap a lot of otherwise useful energy. Concentrate on whatever you take up, and temporarily forget about your other activities.

When you teach your subordinates to be self-sufficient, they will not disturb you for unimportant details. Teach them how to communicate effectively. When they come to you with a problem, let them bring a complete analysis of the same, and also a possible solution if they have one to suggest. This way, they will solve many a problem on their own. All that they may require from you is a go ahead signal, saving much of your time in the process.

An efficient assistant can be a great asset. The assistant could attend the telephone calls, record messages, meet visitors before sending them to meet you, handle routine correspondence, and attend to several similar details every day.

In any sphere of activity, communications and papers of all descriptions play an important part. Organize an efficient system of keeping important papers on file. Ensure that you get a paper when you want it. That is exactly what a good system of record keeping should achieve.

People who desire success make their work interesting. Never let monotony set in. That would be the beginning of boredom and fatigue. Mix different kinds of work to avoid boredom. This also keeps the mind alert. Avail of brief periods of rest particularly when there is a rush of work. Tension builds up faster during the rush of work, but rest soon relieves it.

One derives great satisfaction and strength from orderly work. Each success prepares a person for the next success. As a part of an efficient schedule ensure no unattended work is left on your table each evening. If something needs to be postponed for some reason, do not place it in the cold storage. At the end of each week, review all pending matters. Once a month follow this with a thorough check-up of your desk drawers for anything you might have inadvertently tucked away. Do not ignore anything.

Do not look at the end of the day as yet another day got over with. Be enthusiastic about the success achieved that day. Look forward to the wonderful evening that lies ahead to be spent with the family. This can be the best time of the day. Do not take any work home. After a full day's work, you will not be able to tackle it efficiently. If you do make a great effort to get over it, you may have one job completed, but may have other problems in return.

In the evening, do the things you like best. Take the family to a movie or to the club, watch television, or hear your favourite music. You could visit friends, or take some time off for your hobbies. You could prefer to just have a quiet time with the family. Recreation activities help relieve the tension and stress built up during the day. Take full advantage of relaxation. Look forward to a peaceful night's sleep, and yet another wonderful day ahead.

Think it over...

There is an easier, better and quicker way to do most everything. And now as never before, we must check those easier, better, quicker ways and methods.

— *Gustav Metzman*

EFFICIENCY AIDS

We live in an electronic age where computer-aided gadgets dominate the homes and the workplace. The mobile phones, electronic diaries, computers, email and the websites have changed the way people think and act. To promote personal efficiency, one must take advantage of every efficiency aid that a person can learn to use.

Since the modern gadgets are not within the reach of everyone, we cannot ignore the aids already in use to promote efficiency. There are many available in the market. Most of the time, people adapt aids to personal needs. A diary, which can be used to record appointments, important data, reminders to be sent, and such similar information, is an aid that is both useful and popular. People who rely upon their memory rather than a diary should be labelled overconfident. They are really overestimating the memory.

A scribbling pad with a small pencil or pen tied to it is a very useful aid. You could have such pads on your working table, near your telephone at home, in your bedroom, or in any other place where you think you could benefit from it. Some keep a little pad in their pocket or bag. This way the important information can always be transferred to a permanent place when convenient.

An address book is an efficiency aid where you can list the names, addresses and telephone numbers of business associates, friends and those who matter. It is an ideal place to locate names and addresses whenever you might require them. Some prefer to maintain a list of birthdays and wedding anniversaries to facilitate the sending of greetings in time. If your business or profession requires it, you could maintain a bigger version of an address book by having a classified mailing list. However, it is necessary to revise the address book or the mailing lists periodically to keep them up to date. Many people are using digital diaries, or the home computer, to record this information.

Visiting cards, trays to accommodate papers and files that are coming to you or going out, ball pens and pencils of varying colours to mark correspondence and documents, an intercom phone, and a whole lot of similar items are used to promote efficiency inside and outside the office. You could adapt them to suit your own needs. You should always be on the lookout for ideas you can use to promote personal efficiency.

RELAXATION AND EFFICIENCY

On attaining success, most people strive harder to continue to attain still greater success. The pleasure and satisfaction from success is enough to take their minds away from other needs. Time becomes short to attain all of what lies ahead. In the process, most people begin to ignore their needs of rest, relaxation and sleep. This amounts to breaking the rules of nature. Despite the fact that the physical self refuses to cope with the additional stress, most people continue to place a greater burden on their system, eventually paying a heavy price for it.

One works through the muscles, which contract, or relax, depending upon the need. The longer they are put to work, the longer they remain contracted. This causes tension in the adjacent nerves, which together with the wear and tear in the muscles, causes fatigue. People try several different measures to overcome this fatigue. Stimulating drinks like tea, coffee, or alcoholic beverages, massage, drugs, and physical rest are all intended to overcome fatigue. Of all the ways used, the best way to be relieved of fatigue caused by physical exertion is rest.

It is not that the people are not aware of this simple fact. They rely upon other measures because they do not know how to rest and gain complete relief from the tensions of everyday living.

One must make a special effort to learn the art of physical relaxation. The daily practice makes it a part of one's habits. One must avoid as much physical strain as is possible. It is more restful to walk than to stand, as this gives rest to each leg one by one. Rather than stand, it is more restful to sit. Still better, it is more comfortable to lie down. To promote relaxation, the aim should be to relax the muscles, to loosen the muscle contraction completely. The moment this is achieved, the nerves too become less tense. Mental activity ceases automatically, and is followed by immediate relief.

To make natural relaxation more satisfying, locate areas that tend to get more tired and tense. Then deliberately practise to relax them while lying in bed in an undisturbed room. Let the muscles become limp. With each progressive effort, you will find greater relief. Because of the conscious effort to relax yourself, you will simultaneously develop stress consciousness to avoid strain in the future.

At the workplace, one begins to appreciate the need for comfortable furniture, a pleasant atmosphere, and of having a posture, which places the least strain on muscles. It may not be practical to have a bed to rest in the day. However, it will be helpful if you can rest for a short while each day, sitting on a comfortable chair with your eyes closed, and the mind temporarily at rest. Learning the art of physical relaxation will enhance mental relaxation too. It will make you more efficient and successful.

SUCCESS AND LIFESTYLE CHANGES

When you succeed, you will need to change your lifestyle so that it is in harmony with the lifestyle of the people you move with. It may be all right to wear jeans and a tee shirt at home, but at work you may be expected to be in a shirt and trousers, and perhaps, even wear a necktie. In the winters, you may be expected to wear a suit, or a combination jacket.

Here are a few questions that you will need to answer as you adopt a lifestyle that is yours, and not copied:

1. What kind of an image would you like to project of yourself?
2. Do you stand straight? Or do you slouch?
3. Do you shave everyday? Or do you wear a beard? Is the beard well maintained?
4. Are your hair well trimmed to suit your personality?
5. Are you known to be neatly dressed? Are your clothes clean and well ironed? Are they well matched? Do you wear necktie and socks to match?
6. Are your shoes neat and well polished?
7. Do you wear clothes that are suitable for the occasion?
8. Do the clothes fit you well?
9. Do you have enough variety in your wardrobe?
10. Are you particular about your accessories? Wristwatch? Handkerchief? Wallet? Briefcase? Sunglasses?

11. Do you replace your clothes periodically, adding a few every few months, and giving away the old ones?
12. Does it embarrass you if you were to open your wardrobe before others? Or is it always well maintained?

The home is also a symbol of a person's success. Success is visible in different forms within the home. Here are a few questions that could help you:

1. Does your home reflect your success?
2. Is your house neat and clean? Or are you hesitant to invite people to your home?
3. Are the toilets clean and well maintained?
4. Is the furniture well maintained?
5. Do you buy things because they are status symbols, or because you need and use them?
6. Are all the appliances in your home used regularly?

> **Think it over...**
>
> There is a great man who makes everyone feel small. But the really great man is the man who makes every man feel great.
>
> *— G.K. Chesterton*

SHARING SUCCESS

When you succeed, and enjoy the top position, people will look forward to meet you, and also be invited for a meal, or a party on special occasions. As a successful person, it will be expected that your parties will be special.

Here are a few ways to make your parties memorable:

- Greet each guest individually on his or her arrival. This will make them feel welcome.
- If some of the guests are new to each other, introduce them to each other.
- Ensure that the guests are able to meet freely. If anyone of them does not have company, or is bored and lonesome, introduce the person to a group or a person of similar interest.
- Make sure that you spend some time with each guest. It makes them feel important. Ask them if they are enjoying themselves, or require something.
- Ensure that drinks and snacks are served to all the guests. Personally look into the service.
- If alcoholic drinks are served, ensure that the last drink is served in time.
- Serve the food in time. The food must be adequate, warm and suitable for both vegetarians and non-vegetarians. Respect individual eating habits.
- Do not insist on prolonging the party. Close it in time. Handle those who overstay with tact and care.
- Thank the guests when they leave. Do not prolong the parting conversation.
- See the guests off at the door.

POINTS TO PONDER

1. One can rise up the ladder of success only step by step.

2. Use criticism as a tool to gain further success. Never let it discourage you.
3. When only a few attain success, one feels lonely in high positions.
4. To remain at the top, keep striving for success. Avoid procrastination.
5. Over-confidence can be misleading.
6. Fatigue and stress follow success. Learn to cope with them.
7. Try to create a fair balance of success in every area of life.
8. Learning to make decisions is important to maintain success.
9. Success and efficiency are linked. Organize your life for efficient living.
10. Adopt as many efficiency aids as is practical.
11. Use relaxation to promote efficiency.
12. Change your lifestyle as you succeed in life.
13. Share your success with others.

NOTES